Pyrenean Dogs

Pyrenean Dogs

Ch DUCONTE &
J.-A. SABOURAUD

*Translated by Diane Powell
and Alan Harwood*

Kaye & Ward : Kingswood

Text copyright © 1967 by Ch Duconte
and J-A Sabouraud

Translation © 1982 by Diane Powell

First published in Great Britain by
Kaye & Ward Ltd
The Windmill Press
Kingswood, Tadworth, Surrey
1983

0 7182 2290 3

Typeset by John Smith, London
Printed in Great Britain at
The University Press at Cambridge

Contents

Dedicated to the memory of
Monsieur Senac-Lagrange,
who has done so much for the Pyrenean
Dogs, and all of whose notes that were
available have been assembled here

We refer also to the studies of
Messrs Byasson, Dretzen, Dhers,
Dr Dutrey, Paul Mégnin and others
and also add some advice on breeding,
hygiene and training which will be
useful to the novice.

Foreword

This book is concerned with two distinct breeds of dog which, in their native Pyrenean mountains, are working partners. One of them, the little Pyrenean Sheepdog, is quite unknown in Britain.

The other breed, the Pyrenean Mountain Dog, has been here for a long time — Queen Victoria had one in about 1848, and she was not the first. The breed became firmly established in the mid-1930s when that formidable and memorable lady Mme Jeanne Harper Trois-Fontaines began to import and breed it; she continued to do so until her death in 1972.

Since the middle 1960s, indeed, the Pyrenean Mountain Dog has been one of the most popular of the Giant Breeds in Britain. It is the beloved companion of some thousands of families and has achieved the highest honours in the esoteric world of dog-showing, where Bergerie Knur was Supreme Best in Show at Cruft's Dog Show in 1970 and Champion Briarghyll Falstaff, in 1975, was simultaneously Dog of the Year in one nation-wide competition and Top Dog in another.

Nevertheless most British breeders of the Pyrenean Mountain Dog have been strangely unheeding of the French provenance of their breed. Of course they knew it was French; but until recently few visited France to see what the French dogs looked like, whether in the show ring or at home in the mountains.

For most of the time in which the Pyrenean Mountain Dog has been popular in the English-speaking world, there has been little communication with its country of origin. There has in fact been much more contact among British, American, Canadian, South African, Australian,

New Zealand and even Indian and Japanese breeders than between any of them and France. Small wonder that the breed in those countries, in some of which it is much more numerous than in its homeland, has developed along lines which differ considerably from what the French breeders regard as the ideal.

Within the last few years, however, there have been welcome indications that this inexplicable barrier (which is by no means entirely a language barrier) is dissolving. Not only are foreign breeders becoming more attentive to what French breeders are saying and doing, but the French themselves are becoming more eager to be heard abroad. For some ten years and 29 issues until October 1981, when it ceased publication, Sonya Larsen's *International Great Pyrenees Review* provided from Detroit a platform from which French Pyrenean lovers might address the English-speaking world, and they made good use of it. The French Club *La Réunion des Amateurs de Chiens Pyrénéens* now has members in many countries outside France. In the last two or three years many more British enthusiasts have visited France, particularly the Pyrenees; and the attendance at the French "Pyrenean Specials" bids fair to become as international as the crowd round the Pyrenean Ring at Cruft's Dog Show each year.

There are even signs that some of us foreigners might be ready to admit the possibility that the French may perhaps know as well as anyone else what a native French breed should be like (which is not to say that everybody necessarily agrees) and French judges have recently been making the decisions at shows in Britain and the United States.

In the midst of this heightened interest in the origin of the Pyrenean Mountain Dog, the appearance of this translation of the fundamental work on the breed is both timely and welcome. Although it is based on the 1981 French edition the text differs not at all from that of 1967 (except for the introduction of the recently revised Breed Standards) and that is perhaps a pity. But although the last 15 years of history are thus ignored by the book, such matters hardly relate to the breed itself, but only to the people who concern themselves with it. The immutable canine truths are here, as valid today as when they were printed in 1967 or, indeed, as in the years between Crécy and Agincourt when Pyreneans served Gaston Phoebus and the Kings of France half a thousand years before Queen Victoria owned one.

Much of the book is concerned with the Pyrenean Sheepdog. Our French friends say it is the smallest of all sheepdogs (it isn't); it surely is among the cheekiest-looking! There are one or two in South Africa, possibly elsewhere outside France, but none in Britain. It is tempting to hope that they might be introduced here, but we must remember that they are a working breed with a current job (unlike the Mountain Dog whose traditional work is seldom needed nowadays in Britain) and in France they are bred to do their job professionally with-out much in the way of social graces. It would be a pity if this specialised breed, so well fitted for its hardworking mountain life, were to lose its character by adapting to the comparative indolence of British domesticity.

In conclusion: I welcome this book not only for its information about two magnificent breeds but also for the insight it gives into the way our French friends look upon and think about their dogs. It does not seem very different from our own!

Alan R. Harwood,
Secretary,
The Pyrenean Mountain Dog Club of Great Britain.
Chessington,
April 1983.

The
Pyrenean
Mountain
Dog

The Pyrenean Mountain Dog

Honour to whom honour is due. Majestic and elegant in his sumptuous white fur, this son of the mountains is in every respect a great lord as well as an affectionate companion and a formidable guardian, whose vigilance never ceases.

Origins of the Breed

Where does this dog, which is inseparable from the Pyrenean landscape, come from?

The late M. Senac-Lagrange, who collected, examined and condensed all the information already obtained by Messrs Byasson, Bourdette, Doublet, Cayot and Mégnin, has left documentation of which we shall make full use. The Pyrenean Mountain Dog, who in his region of origin is nicknamed 'Patou', probably has an origin as old as the pastoral industry in the mountains.

It seems certain that the mountain dog does not originate in Europe, as one cannot find any trace of it in the fossilised deposits of the Bronze Age. How did he get there? That remains a mystery.

It is impossible to follow what happened to him through the years, but the mountain dog race, or to be more exact the different varieties in which this race re-appeared, (Alpine dogs, Abruzzi dogs, Pyrenean dogs, of which the Tibetan Mastiff seems to be the common ancestor) seem to have confined themselves to their own mountains. At least, this was the fate of the Pyrenean until the end of the 17th century, where we find the first documents to tell us anything reliable about his locality.

However, American dog fanciers think that as early as the beginning of the 16th century, Pyreneans were taken to Newfoundland by the Basque fishermen. They were crossed with black retrievers imported by the English immigrants, which produced the Newfoundland and the Labrador. It has been established that in 1622, the year when the English settled in Newfoundland, there was not a single dog on the island.

This opinion is held by certain foreign dog fanciers, and even more recently, around 1925, we received a request from an Englishman, a Newfoundland breeder, for Pyreneans to cross with his dogs to strengthen them.

The information we have on the common ancestry of the Tibetan mastiff indicates that this dog was fawn, brown or black. However, when our dog arrived in the Pyrenees he had already spent years and years in the plains and in the mountains, subjected to notable variations in climate and environment, and even in the Pyrenees, with its milder climate and different luminosity, he underwent a great change in the colour of his coat. M. Charles Douillard noticed in the museum at the Château de Lourdes two 19th century engravings in which the dogs depicted have a brown head and even a thick brown coat – this coat has progressively disappeared – the brown has faded to become blaireau or a dirty yellow colour, existing only on the head, with certain patches, notably at the root of the tail. The pure white is now in great demand, possibly to the detriment of pigmentation.

His habits, his character, his employment

Throughout the centuries the Pyrenean shepherds, for security reasons, used this faithful companion to defend themselves and their flocks against attacks by wolves and bears. Throughout the night, while the flock and the shepherd were asleep, 'Patou', having arrived at the resting place or in the part of the mountain chosen by the shepherd for him to stay, would climb onto a raised rock from where he could survey his surroundings. He no

longer tried to follow his master, who would go on to the hut, but would lie down and, with his head stretched out on his paws, could observe anything that might happen near the flock. Could he foresee danger? He can recognise a dangerous situation and would bark to warn the shepherd. If necessary he would fight to protect the flock. Filled with insurmountable courage, and backed up by his formidable strength and powerful jaws, nothing could stop him and nothing would make him retreat. To avoid serious accidents in these struggles with wild animals, the dogs were armed with special collars to protect the throat.

The following is a description of an old collar for Pyreneans: of rigid construction, made of iron, 9 cms wide, and armed with conical spikes 3 cm long, the clasp is secured by a sliding pin fastened at one end by a screw. There were also narrower, flexible collars, an example of which we saw long ago. The exterior spikes were twisted at the base, forming links which fitted together. This type of collar seems to have been less widely used than the rigid collar, without doubt because it was less protective. We have never seen a solid iron collar in the Pyrenees, such as are depicted on certain old engravings around the necks of mastiffs hunting wild animals and wild boars.

This dog, which seems so gentle, becomes a terrible opponent to anything daring to attack the flock that he is guarding. He no longer recognises anyone, will not be stroked or accept titbits; he is occupied solely with his sheep and nothing will divert his vigilant attention. Often he will appear to be sleeping, but he is not, you can be sure of that. Once night falls he will not stop barking to warn everyone that he is on guard; he will not rest for a moment, but will scour his surroundings without ever straying too far, unless he picks up the scent of a dangerous prowler, in which case he will follow it and return only when he feels that his distance from the flock will be a danger to it. The true Pyrenean Mountain Dog should never sleep during the night; his time for resting and sleeping is during the day.

What distinguishes the Pyrenean Mountain Dog from

the other strongly built breeds is his keen sense of smell, his good temper, his attachment to everything that he is given to guard, his devotion to his master.

Here is an example of this attachment and faithfulness.

In 1960 M. Delattre sold *Irving de Pontoise* to Mme Harper as a puppy. During a visit in 1961, M. Delattre had the opportunity to spend some time stroking this dog, who was now fully grown. He returned to England four years later, in 1965, on the occasion of Crufts Dog Show, on an organised trip, during which it was planned to visit the Kennels of Mme Harper, who very kindly received forty Frenchmen. While they were there, to their great surprise, Irving literally threw himself into the arms of M. Delattre when he went into his kennel. M. Delattre was deeply moved by this proof of fidelity, which he was not expecting.

We could give hundreds of similar anecdotes.

To prove the guarding qualities of the Pyrenean, M. Byasson describes the history of the Château de Foix. This castle stands on a rocky escarpment and is not readily accessible, comprising a prison and dungeons which were constantly filled with thieves, highwaymen and bandits, who stopped and robbed all travellers passing through this country into Spain, and who also plundered the flocks in the mountains who did not have a particularly safe guard. The number of these highway-men became so great that it was difficult to accommodate them in prisons. There were no longer enough guards to watch over them so that they had to add a certain number of Pyrenean Mountain Dogs, whose great quali-ties of a keen sense of smell and nocturnal vigilance were already causing a stir in those days. As protection against these plunderers, the shepherds had for some time trained their faithful guardians to chase them in the same way that they chased wild animals. So Foix had its guard of Pyreneans, and from that day Foix was well protected. How could it have been otherwise with watchdogs endowed with such a marvellous instinct that they could recognise wrongdoers by their clothes and never attacked anyone whose appearance was that of an honest person. Clothing today can so often be deceptive,

but the quality of clothing in those days was a precious thing and was never used as a disguise; clothes literally 'made the man.' There was one occasion, however, when this was not the case and the affair very nearly turned out badly. That was the day when an officer of the castle, wishing to put the shrewdness of the guard dogs to the test, disguised himself as a highwayman and did his night round. He was surrounded by the raging dogs, knocked down in an instant and fortunately, as he was struggling under their paws, he was recognised by the brave beasts. One might have thought this an old legend without foundation if the researches of the historian J. Bourdette had not enabled us to verify its authenticity.

We notice in his work on the Château de Lourdes, which was the result of a document he found in the National Library, that in 1407 this castle had a square tower and a round tower which were protected by a wall, and between the towers and the wall there was a pathway where the Pyreneans walked to do their night patrol, and if necessary to raise the alarm. Bearing in mind the fact that the Seigneurs of Foix were Counts of Bigorre, and as such owners of Lourdes, we can assume that all the châteaux that came under their ownership had their guard of Pyreneans, and that this position of trust was reserved for them; such was the great confidence that one had in their qualities.

An even older document found in the archives of Foix tells how in 1391, in consequence of a treaty on the subject of the succession of Gaston Phoebus, Count of Foix, King Charles VI decided to pay a visit to his cousin, who was expecting him at his château at Mazéres. Before arriving at Mazéres the King passed through a region full of white cows wearing silver bells around their necks. Knights, acting as herdsmen, were running round trying to clear a way through the herd. Some enormous mountain dogs were helping them when a bull charged at the King. One of the herdsmen seized the bull by the horns and turned it round while the dogs, hanging onto its ears, made it go back to the herd, thus saving the King.

We can therefore claim that for centuries this breed has always been considered as the ideal guard dog, as well as a charming companion. This can be seen in the gentle contemplative look in his dark eye, his air of searching the mountain, which can neither be explained nor described but which belongs only to him – the 'Pyrenean expression'. It was this that gained him the favour of the young Dauphin of France in 1675. At that time Mme de Maintenon accompanied the young Dauphin to Barèges. While out walking, the child met a beautiful 8-month old Patou, to which he gave titbits. The two became inseparable, so much so that the Dauphin suggested that Patou should leave his mountain to live at the Louvre, and that is how the Pyrenean became the royal dog.

Two years later the Marquis de Louvois went to Barèges and also wanted a Pyrenean. He acquired a one year old at Betpouey; the animal was remarkably beautiful and received the admiration of the entire court. From that moment the Pyrenean gained the favour of the nobility, and anyone who owned a castle with beautiful grounds wanted a lovely Patou.

So through the centuries this was the double role of the lord in white fur; that of faithful companion to the mountain shepherds in times of relative security, and to keep highwaymen wolves and bears at bay.

The progressive disappearance of these predators was to have inevitable repercussions on the existence and prosperity of the Pyrenean Mountain Dog. Their number diminished. Then thoughtless exportation finally made the state of the breed precarious. The north of France, Belgium and England took a considerable number of puppies. The number was so great that unscrupulous profiteers left no stone unturned and sold many dogs of doubtful origin as purebred dogs.

As with all breeds, and perhaps more than any other, the 1914 war finally had a profound disturbance on the breeding of Pyreneans. Many dogs were killed; the survivors, badly nourished as a result of rationing, did not always reach the necessary standard and after the war were not fit for breeding purposes.

To prevent it being ultimately jeopardised, it was necessary that the interests of the Pyrenean Mountain Dog should be officially taken in hand by a group of devoted lovers of the breed. It was at Lourdes, on the outskirts of the pleasant, yet imposing Labeda region, the home of our breed, that an official group called the Réunion des Amateurs de Chiens Pyrénéens endeavoured to maintain the breeding of Pyreneans on a rational basis. A thankless task to perform with limited means, in the midst of a general indifference, often hindered further by ignorance and greed.

Even before this, attempts had been made in this same region to remedy disturbances to breeding. In 1907, thanks to the efforts of Dr Moulonget, M. Camajou and M. Senac-Lagrange, the Pastour Club was founded under the presidency of Baron A. de la Chevrelière. During the same year as its foundation, this group managed at one particularly successful show, to gather together the remarkable number of 53 dogs in a class for adult males, a record number that has never been reached since at a show in France or abroad. At the beginning of July 1907 the Pastour Club also had the honour of bringing out the first Pyrenean standard, the authors of which were the founders of the club. In the same year, 1907, following a journey in cynological studies undertaken by the Count of Bylandt and Th Dretzen, a Pyrenean Mountain Dog club was founded at Argelès-Gazost, initiated by M. E. Byasson, an ardent lover and breeder of Pyreneans. These gentlemen were, perhaps, a little dogmatic in their conclusions in declaring:

> Having visited the Pyrenean regions of Pau, Bagnères-de-Bigorre, Bagnères-de-Luchon, Tournay, Lourdes, Gavarnie, Cauterets and Argelès-Gazost with a view to examining on the spot the main qualities and peculiarities which make up the pure bred Pyrenean Mountain Dog, and having made investigations and a detailed examination of all the subjects that were shown to us, and that we were able to meet in the course of our peregrinations, we certify and attest that the cradle of this breed is Argelès-Gazost and that there alone can one still find perfect examples of the pure breed.

Thank God we can now see beautiful subjects outside this restricted area.

M. Dretzen, who was very enthusiastic about the beauty of these dogs, took several home with him to form the basis of his breeding stock. He had the most practical, most hygienic and most elegant kennels that one has ever seen built at his house at Colombes on the outskirts of Paris. So as to keep the muscles of his Pyreneans toned up – he had up to twelve – he employed a former sergeant of the Chasseurs Alpins, who took them every morning for a brisk walk lasting three hours at infantryman's pace!

The dispersion of sincere and devoted lovers of the breed, who had taken the interests of the Pyrenean Mountain Dog in hand, meant that the action of the groups that we have been speaking about had only a relative effect, as it was too ephemeral and diminished after a lapse of several years. Undoubtedly the lack of clear directives on breeding was one of the predominant causes of the eclipse suffered by the breed.

In 1927 M. Senac-Lagrange wrote the following reflections:

It is without doubt that the canine breeds, however they have evolved, cannot exist without the help of groups of supporters in the form of specialised breed clubs. Through what changes must the lord in white fur now pass? What will be his future? Undoubtedly that of all the large canine breeds.

In an age when fashion seems to turn more and more towards the small dog; in times when the qualities of a guard dog are utilised less and less, it is permissible to think that whatever the efforts undertaken to make it known and appreciated, the breeding of the Pyrenean Mountain Dog has little chance of increasing to any great extent. Outside its country of origin it will rest in the hands of an elite, anxious simply to own and maintain this magnificent dog in its prime beauty.

In 1967 the situation does not seem to be the same at all. It would seem rather that it is in the homeland of the breed that its production has diminished. Outside the two regions of the Pyrenees and Ariège we can find very select breeding in various regions of France. In England, thanks to the impetus given by Mme Harper, president of the Pyrenean Mountain Dog Club of Great Britain, our large dogs are very widespread. There is a specialised club in America, and there are numerous lovers of the breed throughout the whole world, where they have acclimatised themselves quite well.

M. Senac-Lagrange insists on the following points: the Pyrenean is a highly characterised dog, at least amongst the large European breeds. The Leonberg dog seems to be the only one which by its morphological characteristics approaches it. Is it possible to believe that these two dogs had a common ancestry? What is certain is that one can detect both dogs, without any appreciable modification to their format, their general appearance and their temperament on the high plateaux of Anatolia and in certain parts of Macedonia. We have found them in the first of these regions in the hands of Turkish shepherds, who employed them to guard their flocks against the wolves that infested the country. They were large dogs,

70 – 75cm high (28 – 30in), with a white coat, marked on the head only with patches of reddish grey. Everything about these dogs reminded us of the Pyrenean, from their gait, their tail carriage, their rather hoarse bark to the way they behaved towards the flock. The only difference, which is accounted for by the difference in climate, was that whilst their fur was the same colour and texture as that of the Pyrenean, it was shorter.

One of our friends, an informed dog fancier, told us that he had met identical dogs in the mountainous part of Macedonia, in the vicinity of Gornitchevo. Finally, however, there also exists in Anatolia a dog with a striking resemblance to the Leonberg. We personally had one dog, whose photograph we still have, who in a show ring was described as a very typical Leonberg dog. This would seem to confirm the general opinion which attributes an Asiatic origin to mountain dog breeds, which would have been introduced into Europe at the time of the invasions. The likeness between the Leonberg and the Pyrenean is undeniable. The well known painting of the ideal Leonberg by Allemand A. Kull could, except perhaps for a slightly accentuated curve of the skull, pass for a typical Pyrenean. M. P. Megnin in his work *The Dog and its Species* published a reproduction of a photograph of a Leonberg dog which resembles a true Pyrenean.

We believe that no attempt has been made in France to cross the Leonberg with the Pyrenean. However, if a crossing should one day be tried as a desperate attempt by breeders to strengthen the breed, it is between the Leonberg and the Pyrenean that it should be attempted.

The attempts made in this respect with the St Bernard did not give the results that were hoped for. The breeders had hoped for some interesting results from the crossing of animals raised in similar surroundings, having even a common ancestry, since the monks of the Hospice of St Bernard claimed that their breed of dog was the result of crossing a mastiff with a Pyrenean bitch. The results did not come up to their expectations. The products of the crossing had lost the majestic elegance, characteristic of pure-bred Pyreneans. The most obvious results of these attempts were that the heads were foreshortened and became heavy; enlarged parietal bones, accentuated zygomatics, a more defined stop, a general slackening of tissues and even a change in the almost indefinable Pyrenean expression, which is tender, contemplative and even a little sad all at the same time, and which the old mountain herdsmen called the 'Pyrenean look'.

The dogs on the Spanish side of the Pyrenees differ somewhat to those on the French side. In general they are less typical. They are taller, their fur is generally less abundant, sometimes appearing to be close cropped, and quite often the coat has brighter colours – the pale yellow becomes orange and the blaireau grey becomes black. The skull is more curved and the sides of the head are more rounded. In certain dogs it can be suspected that there has been an infusion of blood of the old Spanish 'perro de presa'.

The effect of any crossing with the Pyrenean, therefore, shows itself with regularity in the enlargement of the skull and broadening of the muzzle. Thus the opinion of the German naturalist Brehm, who classes the Pyrenean amongst dogs of the wolf type, should not be thought of as being absolutely fantastic, as one is tempted to do with the actual state of the breed today (1927). He considers the Pyrenean, together with the Alpine dog and the Abruzzi dog as varieties of one breed.

In 1967 we can take it that all attempts at crossing are finished. The breed is well fixed, too beautiful to try to modify, and one has only to keep to the carefully established principles of the standard to respect it.

Standard Of The Pyrenean Mountain Dog

General Appearance

That of a dog of great size, imposing and strongly built, but not lacking a certain elegance.

Faults General appearance giving an impression of heaviness, without distinction, or indicating a resemblance to the St. Bernard, the Newfoundland or the Leonberg. Dogs which are fat, sluggish, lymphatic or other than of a dangerous appearance.

Height

Males: 0.70 – 0.80m (28 – 32in)
Females: 0.65 – 0.72m (26 – 28in)

A tolerance of 2cm above is permitted for dogs of a perfect type.

Weight

Male approximately 60kg (132lb)
Female approximately 45kg (100lb).

Head

Not too large in comparison to height. The sides of the head are fairly flat; the skull is slightly arched; the occiputal furrow being apparent, the back of the skull is domed.

The size of the skull at its widest part is equal to its length. It is joined by a gentle slope to a large muzzle, of good length, tapering at its extremity. The slightly drooping lips just cover the lower jaw; they are black or strongly marked with black, as is the palate. The nose is completely black.

Faults Head too heavy; skull too developed; forehead arched; noticeable division of the nose; mucous membranes insufficiently pigmented; lips drooping too much; rectangular shaped head.

Elimination The whole nose of a colour other than absolutely black.

Teeth

There should be a complete set of teeth, the teeth clean and white. The incisors of the upper jaw cover those of the lower jaw, without ever losing contact with them (figure No. 4). A pincer bite is permitted (fig. 3).

Elimination Projecting lower jaw (fig. 2) or upper jaw (fig. 1).

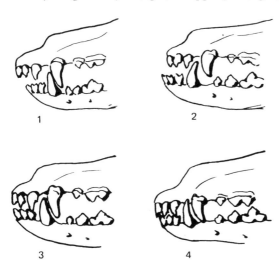

Eyes

The rather small eyes, with an intelligent and thoughtful expression, are brown-amber coloured, surrounded by close fitting eyelids, bordered black and set slightly obliquely. The look is soft and dreamy.

Faults Eyes which are round, too pale or protruding; drooping eyelids; vicious or haggard expression. Lack of pigmentation around the eye.

Elimination Scabby eyelids.

Ears

Planted on a level with the eye; fairly small; triangular shaped; rounded at the tips; they fall flat against the head; carried a little higher when the dog is alert.

Faults Ears which are long, curled or doubled over, or fixed too high.

Neck

Strong, fairly short with slightly developed dewlaps.

Faults Slender, rather long, dewlaps too pronounced.

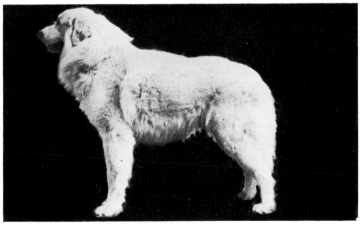

Body

The chest does not slope very much, but is large and deep. The sides are gently rounded. The back is of a good length, broad and straight. The rump slopes slightly, with the haunches fairly prominent.

Faults Topline dipping or arched (see general appearance). Sloping towards the front. Abdomen like that of a greyhound. (Fig. No. 2)

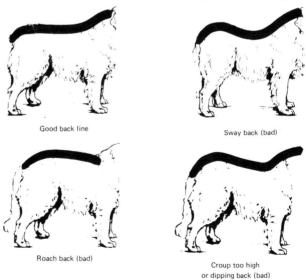

Good back line

Sway back (bad)

Roach back (bad)

Croup too high
or dipping back (bad)

Legs

The front legs are straight, strong and well fringed. Fringes also exist on the hind legs, but longer and thicker. The thighs are strong and slope slightly. The hocks are well boned, lean and of medium angulation. Both hind legs have well-formed double dewclaws.

Faults Straight hocks, cow hocks or knock knees.

Elimination Absence of dewclaws; single dewclaw or double dewclaw not properly formed on the back legs.

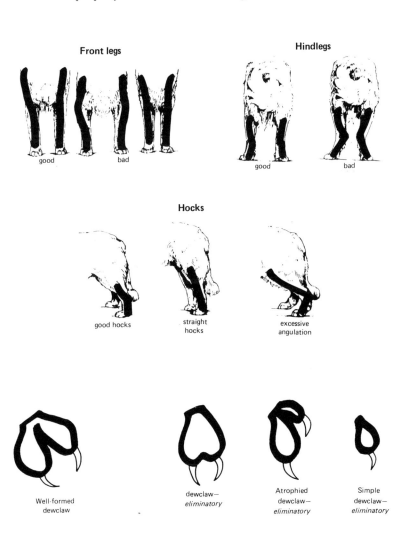

Front legs

good   bad

Hindlegs

good   bad

Hocks

good hocks   straight hocks   excessive angulation

Well-formed dewclaw

dewclaw— *eliminatory*

Atrophied dewclaw— *eliminatory*

Simple dewclaw— *eliminatory*

Feet
Not very long, compact with slightly arched toes.

Faults Feet too long and flat.

Tail
Fairly long, bushy and forming a plume; carried low in repose, preferably with a crook at the tip; when the dog is alert it rises over the back, curling round tightly ('making a wheel' according to the expression of the Pyrenean mountain people).

Faults Insufficient hair on tail or tail badly carried; tail too short or too long, or without a plume; not making a wheel when moving, or making it continually even when at rest.

Fur
Thick and straight; fairly long and soft, longer on the tail and around the neck, where it can wave slightly. The hair on the trousers is finer, more woolly and very thick.

Faults Short or curly hair. Absence of undercoat.

Coat
White or white with patches of grey (or blaireau), or pale yellow or wolf grey or orange on the ears and at the root of the tail. Blaireau patches are preferred. Some dogs have a few patches on the body.

Faults Colours other than those indicated above, which would denote cross breeding.

Elimination Patches of hair which are black to the root.

Gait (Photo 8)
In spite of its height, the Pyrenean Mountain Dog has an easy gait, never giving an impression of heaviness, but on the contrary very elegant; its angulations give it an even gait.

Elimination for Males *Monorchidism* or *cryptorchidism*, i.e. having only one testicle or none at all.

Scale Of Points

Skull and muzzle (nose, lips, jaws)	15
Eyes	10
Ears	5
Neck, Back, Loins, Rump	12
Shoulders, Chest, Sides, Flanks	10
Legs and feet	10
Tail and tail carriage	8
Fur, colour, pigmentation	15
General appearance (expression, height, gait)	15
	100

The main breed points, which are the combined result of the head, coat, colouring, expression and gait, add up to 60 points out of a total of 100. The main indication of the purity of the breeding should never be sacrificed to the perfection of anatomical points, however important they may be. Concerning the general appearance of the Pyrenean, we insist that it does not give the impression of heaviness, which is often the case with large dogs, amongst them the St Bernard, and it is this that has caused us to credit him in the standard as 'a dog not lacking a certain elegance'.

We have already written about the very special expression of the Pyrenean and will not come back to it.

The tail carriage is fairly characteristic of the Pyrenean. A tail constantly carried low on the hocks is the sign of an animal that is cross bred or that is sick. The pure bred dog, and one that is in good health will lift his tail and round it over his back as soon as he is alert. This action is automatic in certain dogs as soon as they start to move. The tail is rounded, but not rolled so that the end of the tail falls on the side level with the loins. This characteristic tail carriage could, however, be the cause of a dog, endowed with many other qualities, failing to gain the first place under an ignorant judge who would describe it as having a 'gay tail'.

The following are two fairly common errors relating to the Pyrenean coat. Certain people imagine that the only orthodox coat is the all white one. On the other hand, others see it as a mark of degeneracy. But both these opinions are wrong.

The white coat is by no means abnormal when the pigment is black. Pure white dogs have become progressively numerous. What is certain is that the dominant colour, the background of the coat, must be white. Too many patches on the body do not relate at all to the original type of Pyrenean. The people in the mountains appreciate dogs that are lightly marked on the head and sometimes at the root of the tail. That is where the provincial expression from Labeda 'U ca pla plapat' (well marked dog) originates.

Pierre Mégnin describes the Pyrenean as almost all white, or white with reddish marks. The Count of Bylandt, in the first edition of his book *Breeds of Dogs* describes the coat as white, sometimes with lemon yellow marks. Bénédict Henri Revoil in his *Physiological and Anecdotic History of Dogs* published in 1867 is more explicit about the colour and describes a dog with white fur streaked with patches of orange, yellow ochre or grey. Finally, Hugh Dalziel, from descriptions given by English tourists, and having seen several specimens taken to England – undoubtedly quite imperfect – gives the Pyrenean coat as a mixture of white, yellow, fawn and black.

34

Regarding height, this seems to have been in a state of regression for a certain number of years already (1927). In 1877 Pierre Mégnin wrote in a paper on acclimatisation, "There is in the Pyrenees, particularly in Ariège, a dog even larger and stronger than the St Bernard", and some years later in his work on the dog, he gave the height for a Pyrenean as 80 – 85 cm (32 – 34 in) or even 90 cm (35½ in). Such specimens cannot be found today and we do not know of any dog reaching 80 cm at the shoulders, the maximum height indicated in the standard.

The measurements taken by us of a fairly large number of dogs 20 years ago, compared to those taken quite recently since the war (1925) enables us to say that the present average height is lower by almost 3 cm than the average before the war (1914), and that the minimum limits indicated in the standard for dogs as well as for bitches exceed the actual average heights by approximately 2 cm.

Although the usefulness of the dewclaws is debatable, they have from time immemorial been a characteristic of the Pyrenean Mountain Dog, and the mountain breeders continue to consider them as a definite sign of purity of breeding. The writers of the standard would, therefore, have done wrongly not to have indicated their absence as an eliminating fault.

We will have finished with these comments once we have added that some Pyreneans have the peculiarity of sometimes adopting a gait which is not that of the broken amble shown in veterinary horse diagrams, and in which the legs on each side move together in four-time.

In dealing with the Pyrenean Sheepdogs, we will have occasion to return to this peculiar gait, which seems to be a gait of adaptation.

We will finish on a psychological and practical note.

We can claim that this breed has, since the earliest times, been considered as an ideal guard dog. His keen sense of smell, intelligence, absolute devotion to his master and to everything that he is given to guard, excessive amenability, wakefulness at night, strength, energy and courage in the face of anything, none of these fails him. Add to that his height, his robust constitution, the strength of his jaws, the majesty of his bearing, the volume of his bark, his thick mane which stands on end when he becomes angry, his surprising agility, the animation of his expression when he foresees danger, and you will realise the services he can render as a guard dog, especially in remote regions.

As to training, none is necessary when it is a matter of guarding. He guards because he was born with this inherited instinct; he guards only that which he loves and he loves only that which he is given to guard. His intellect may not have the vivacity of the sheepdog, but it has the advantage of being backed up by a greater thinking power. Having talked about his devotion and affection, we must mention the case of a child who was met every day by his friend, a Patou, to take and fetch him back from school. The brave dog allowed himself to be mounted like a donkey and very proudly took the child back to his parents at the slow, gentle pace of a mountain shepherd.

If one should wish to give him a special piece of work, it is necessary, as with all dogs, to give him the required training. We will study this in a separate chapter.

In the past our large Pyreneans have been called upon to do a little of every kind of work. In Belgium and in the north of France, harnessed to little carts, they were employed for the distribution of milk or to carry luggage. Smugglers used them to pass their contraband goods. During the 1914 war they were an excellent means of communication. Quite recently we have seen them as film actors. Each week during the winter of 1965–66 everyone admired *Belle and Sebastien* on the television, sometimes with emotion.

Breeding

One does not suddenly become a breeder – one becomes one after study and observation.

Neither must one believe that a dog breeds by itself. If you believe this you are heading straight for disappointments, which show themselves in loss of time and money. We interviewed a specialist on this subject, our friend M. André Delattre, a serious breeder who has successfully bred Pyreneans since 1933 and who was anxious to tell us of his breeding methods.

We will first speak of the stud dog in a general way. Having chosen him, it is necessary to study his pedigree to avoid too much inbreeding. Then it is necessary to examine him carefully from the point of view of the standard and not to find in him the same faults as the bitch may have: to add and multiply faults is not a process for improving the breed. Certainly there is not a perfect dog, but it is not prohibited to try to attain perfection, and for that it is necessary above all to eliminate congenital faults, such as lack of pigmentation, prognathism, to speak only of the most common ones.

When the stud dog is a novice one must have a lot of patience: try to help him if he will allow it. After the coupling it is wise, if the dog has to meet other males, to rub him down with disinfectant, such as 90° alcohol, to remove the scent of the bitch and avoid a fight, dogs being extremely jealous.

Neither dogs nor bitches should be used for reproduction until they are at least two years old. A bitch who is too young risks being deformed by an untimely litter: the back will dip and the hind quarters will not maintain the necessary harmony.

A bitch should not be mated right at the beginning nor right at the end of her season. The best time is from the 9th to the 12th day. It is necessary to worm the bitch beforehand as it must not be forgotten that the worms pass from the mother to her pups via the placenta during the period of gestation. To be sure of a good mating, it is not a bad thing, if possible, to repeat the mating the following day or the day after that – some owners of bitches are not exactly sure about the beginning of the heat and, after all, 'twice is better than once'. It is recommended to let the bitch rest for a while before making her journey home, especially if she is disturbed by the car. As with all breeds, the period of gestation is approximately 62 days.

Returning to M. Delattre. From the end of the third week of gestation, the bitch should be given calcium and vitamins so that she does not have to supply all the elements necessary for the formation of her offspring from her own body, but one should stop the calcium eight days before whelping so that the pups do not have too rigid a skeleton, which would make their birth difficult.

While certain bitches whelp calmly, others who are very nervous do not stay still, disturbing the straw and the pups at the same time. In this case it is wise to leave only one pup and to remove the others as soon as they are born, putting them all back when the last one has arrived, having put them in a warm place in the meantime so that they can dry off and do not catch cold.

There are bitches who are very careful when they lie down with their pups; others, who are heavier or more clumsy, lie down awkwardly and unfortunately for the pup lying underneath, it is inevitable that he will die from suffocation, especially at night. This also happens when the pups begin to crawl around – if they move round their mother or crawl over her, they end up behind her and can become wedged between the wall and the bitch's back. To prevent this one should install an iron rod 20 cm from the wall and 15 cm from the ground, which will leave a free space, a passageway, so that a puppy that finds himself there does not run any risk.

Towards the age of two weeks the puppies' nails are very sharp, and when feeding they will cruelly scratch their mother's teats almost to the point of drawing blood, and she often reacts with the pain, so it is best to cut the ends of the claws with nail scissors.

In the case of an over large litter, should one cull some of the pups? This question has always been much discussed. In principle the mother should be able to feed whatever nature has given her, at least as many pups as she has nipples. However, sometimes our large Pyreneans are extremely fertile, having up to fourteen puppies, or even more. When these bitches have only nine or ten nipples, is it wise to let them have more puppies? If the choice of a pup is difficult at the time of weaning, it is even more difficult on the day of whelping. The smallest could possibly become the most beautiful! Do not be too hasty. Possible accidents may be responsible for reducing the number of pups.

The puppies become increasingly greedy as they grow. It is important to give the mother plenty of good food to cope with this. Some bitches will eat up to 3 kg of meat a day, always with the addition of calcium and vitamins. A well fed bitch should not become thin while she is suckling, and her puppies should double their birth weight in eight days, and triple it in a fortnight.

Towards the age of three weeks one can start teaching them to lap, especially if the litter is large, when the mother will no longer have enough milk to ensure good growth of her puppies. Everything depends on the quality of the mother's milk.

Within three days the puppies should know how to drink; from this time one can mix a thin porridge in with their milk, and a week later start to add a small quantity of chopped meat, increasing the amount gradually.

Almost all puppies have worms – these ascarids, which they do not get rid of easily, and which are not desirable, live in the stomach to the detriment of the puppy. They should be wormed when they are 4 – 5 weeks old, and again every month after.

From the age of three months it is best to have them vaccinated against distemper. Do not vaccinate a puppy that has not been properly wormed against all types of worms several days beforehand. After the puppy starts to eat, add calcium, and vitamins to his food, which are combined in several veterinary products. Above all, do not forget that the dog is carnivorous.

If you wish to develop a good dog, it is necessary to give him raw or grilled meat. At the beginning you can start with 200 g (8 oz) a day of chopped meat with rice and vegetables, building up very quickly to the adult ration recommended by M. Mégnin in 1946:

>Bread: 1 kg
>Meat: 400 – 500 g
>Rice and vegetables: 250 g

The rice should be given boiled and washed.

I think that it is better to insist on rice rather than bread, and above all on vegetables boiled with a large bone – knuckle of veal – which one can give to the dog to chew afterwards. Raw grated carrot is excellent.

Hygiene

We should remember that our long haired dogs need regular attention, which is necessary for their health.

Our first care is to avoid parasites: fleas, lice, ticks. At present there are numerous efficient insecticides. In particular it is best to look for ticks – some are infectious and lethal. They give rise almost immediately to an illness called piroplasmosis, a virus which destroys the red corpuscles in the blood. In its severe form it is easy to recognise. The mucous membranes (nose, lips, eyelids) become white and yellowish. The dog is miserable, refuses all food, passes urine the colour of tobacco juice. In its mild form the symptoms are less apparent. The dog is miserable and off his food. Discolouration of the mucous membranes takes place more slowly. This form is even more dangerous.

We will not undertake to describe all the illnesses that can beset a dog. One word of advice – do not wait until he is ready to die before taking him to the vet.

Each day you should brush him carefully with a stiff brush and comb him gently with a metal comb to prevent the formation of knots. Take great care at the time of moulting to remove the dead fur.

It is better not to wash him but to maintain the whiteness and cleanliness of the fur with an occasional dry shampoo. When it is raining, if he is wet when he returns from his walk, dry him with warm towels and brush him afterwards.

As your dog must be exercised for at least half an hour morning and evening, whatever the weather, he must walk on the lead and must not become fat. Muscle yes, fat no! One can only prevent it by work and exercise.

In the country, the dog running free takes sufficient exercise. I am thinking of the dogs in Paris and in other towns. If you are young, take your bicycle and take your companion for a good walk at a moderate speed. In winter, make sure he does not catch cold when he comes back. Wash his paws with warm water and dry them, then do not leave him in a draught. Avoid keeping your dog on a lead, or as little as possible. A park is best if you cannot let him run completely free.

Training

Above all your dog should be obedient. Obedience is the key to all training, whatever the object of this training and the dog should work happily to give satisfaction to his master. The fear of painful blows paralyses the dog's faculties. With an intelligent dog, kindness is worth more than brutality.

"Time and patience do more than strength and temper".

Let us speak simply for the sake of every dog-lover who wishes to make a companion of their dog, but to have one who is faithful, obedient and clean.

It is when the puppies begin to go out and romp about that it is necessary to educate them. It is at the moment when you have just bought him, after weaning, when he arrives at your home, be it in the town or country, from the first day that you must teach him the principle of cleanliness.

In the country there is no problem. If the puppy forgets himself in the living room when he is with you, show him what he has just done (make sure you put his nose in it) and take him outside saying, "Naughty, not here, go outside". Very soon he will go to the door when he needs to. Open it quickly for him and he will relieve himself outside. Praise him and give him a reward. In less than a week he will understand. Generally the need makes itself particularly felt after meals. If you have him in a flat, give him a shallow box full of sawdust – instead of putting him outside, you can carry him to the box. This box must be in a place where he can reach it at any time. It takes a bit longer to get him into the habit.

From the first days accustom your puppy to wearing a collar and to follow you on a lead. Take him out as often as possible to satisfy his needs. This exercise also helps the bowel movements, especially if the dog is free to run and to come into contact with scents which encourage him. Where a dog has satisfied his needs, all others who pass by will do the same.

You should still be on the lookout if your dog, although very clean at home, goes into the home of another dog – he could well lift his leg against a piece of furniture out of spite or jealousy. At that moment he deserves a good hiding.

When taking him out on the lead, make sure that your dog walks at your side, behind rather than in front, and at the same pace as you; when he is fully grown a hand on his neck should suffice to check him. The principle for getting him to come to you is very simple. If he does not come at the first call, go towards him without being angry and give him a titbit. You will see from the result that it will not take him long to come to you in search of something he likes. Cheese is an excellent enticement. When he is used to it, making a fuss of him will suffice. It is necessary to make him do this from infancy. Progressively you will train him to sit beside you and to wait without moving if you have something to look at or someone to talk to.

Some of our large dogs have an independent nature. Don't put up with anything from the very beginning. You must be the absolute master, but remember that it is not by punishment that you will get a good recall.

If you want special training, such as to know the syllabus of a police dog, join one of the clubs having specialised instructors.

For some unknown reason, the Pyrenean Mountain Dog is not included amongst the dogs allowed to take part in guard dog competitions.

The
Pyrenean
Sheepdog

The Pyrenean Sheepdog

At the risk of repeating ourselves, we think we must refer to studies which have already been published on the origins, character and use of our little sheepdogs (Bergers) which, being written by various people, complement each other and instruct us in a very interesting way. M. Mégnin writes:

In 1927 the veterinary surgeon Louis Dutrey of Rabastens de Bigorre based his doctorate thesis on this subject: *The origin of a breed of dog; the Pyrenean Sheepdog*. This thesis, remarkable in all aspects despite having been drawn from a fairly large number of examples, has been out of print for a very long time, and the lovers of this breed, which is so useful and so intelligent, can find information only in old numbers of our periodical, *L'Eleveur (The Breeder)*, or in certain works in which the authors devote a few pages to the Pyrenean Sheepdog.

Before 1914 this dog was completely unknown outside its region of habitat; in the south western shows one saw only Labrits, which are not Pyrenean Sheepdogs but dogs from Landes. The Labrit is exclusively a lowland dog. The Pyrenean Sheepdog is both a mountain and a lowland dog.

When Commander Malric and Sub-lieutenant Mégnin were put in charge of the Military Dog Service in 1916, both of them thought of the Pyrenean Sheepdog. Endowed with an acute sense of smell, it makes it an ideal dog for communication as well as to accompany patrols. In addition, the Military Dog Service entrusted M. Th Dretzen, a fine expert and handler of sheepdogs, with a mission in the Pyrenees with a view to recruiting as many of these dogs as possible. M. Dretzen brought back a large number of them – I do not need to mention here the very great and very real service rendered by these brave and intelligent little creatures. It was only in 1926 that the Pyrenean Sheepdog was recognised by the French Kennel Club and by the Ministry of Agriculture, and the breed was admitted to the Central General Agricultural Show in the same group as the other varieties of sheepdog.

From then on the Pyrenean Sheepdog achieved a certain amount of success with dog lovers, who bought it and raised it both as a guard dog and as a companion.

The standard was drawn up, recognising two varieties. One, whose general head shape resembled that of a brown bear, with a wedge shaped muzzle; the other with a smooth face and shorter hair on the body. What I would like to point out is the fact that some devotees of the breed have been astonished to learn of some differences in height. The standard allows a range of 10 cm in height.

M. Mégnin remarked that J. Dhers, in an article which appeared in the journal *Le Chien (The Dog)* (Lausanne) wrote:

Although the breed is very clearly established and defined, it is said in our mountains that the types vary a little from valley to valley. The standard remains the same, but certain small details do not escape the mountain dog fanciers. It is thus that the dog from Arbazzie would be the ideal of the standard. The head of the type from Bagnères is something special. The little dog of St-Béat is thick-set, its head round: one could say a miniature bobtail (Old English Sheepdog). The sheepdog of Azun, always black, appears to be a miniature Groenendal.

I must add that the first Pyrenean Sheepdogs to be taken to the Paris region were taken there a few years before 1914, around 1910 or 1911, by a professor of agriculture from Seine-et-Marne, M. Joubert, who had been entrusted with an agricultural mission in the Pyrenees. The three specimens were of the same type, the forehead, including the head, was certainly that of the Pyrenean Sheepdog which we see today, but the hind quarters were very powerful, the stifles well developed and strongly built, the gait was somewhat like that of a brown bear ambling; the coat was that of the present dog; these dogs came from the high region of Ariège.

And now we shall hand the commentary over to M. Dhers:

> A very ancient breed – small dog, pretty little dog, of which an example of a smooth faced type is very accurately depicted in an old publication by Buffon. This alone reduces to nothing the fantastic suppositions written about the Pyrenean Sheepdog by incompetent dog lovers. But pen-sickness is an obstinate itch which afflicts many people. The most

common mistake is that which gives the Briard as being the ancestor of our little sheepdog. And why, if you please? Simply because there is a vague resemblance in the coat and sometimes the colour of these two animals. I say vague resemblance because, to tell the truth, on looking closely the coat of the small Pyrenean is a cross between goat's hair and sheep's wool, which isn't the case with the dog from Brie. But there is more. The general construction, and above all the shape of the skull, are completely different. Finally, the dog from Brie appeared later than the Pyrenean Sheepdog, which I have always seen in our mountains, and which have been in my family for at least three generations, whereas the Briard wasn't really recognised until 1863, the year of the first Paris dog show! For many, the Pyrenean Sheepdog is a new dog because they have only recently known them. It is, in fact, an old indigenous breed which has always remained in its place of origin. There it has always been used to guard the herds of goats, sheep, cows and even horses.

This marvellous dog began to make itself known in the army kennels during the great war of 1914–18, and it was especially appreciated there as a communications dog. After the victory a few Pyrenean dog lovers took it upon themselves to specialise in the breed, to propagate it and to make it known outside its place of origin. They founded a club and established a standard. All their time was occupied by this very interesting variety of sheepdog.

Certain people still designate the Pyrenean Sheepdog under the name of Labrit, or confuse it with the Labrit. It is a mistake, but a mistake which can be explained. Labrit is the name of a principal place in the canton of Landes, and the Labrit is taller than the Pyrenean Sheepdog. But as we have already said, it is a dog belonging to the plains, and has increased in height by living on the plains.

It is said that faith can remove mountains. All the mountain people will tell you, and others too, that the great animator in this case was M. Bernard Senac-Lagrange. The impetus had been given. A second reunion took place at Tarbes and in July 1923 the Réunion des Amateurs de Chiens Pyrénéens (Reunion of Pyrenean Dog Lovers) was founded. M. Senac-Lagrange, the president elect, used all his energy and all his influence with the result that our little Pyrenean Sheepdog, officially recognised, featured in 1926 at the Paris General Agricultural Show, where I had the honour of judging them both that year and the following year.

In my capacity of former training officer in the Military Dog Service, it is my duty to proudly proclaim that it is the Pyrenean Sheepdog which supplied the army with the most intelligent, most knowing, the fastest and most useful communication dogs.

And now, without hesitation, we will return to the long study which M. Senac-Lagrange had inserted in the 1927 year book of the Réunion des Amateurs de Chiens Pyrénéens, and which was published in the club bulletin in 1951.

Officially recognised only recently and unknown to most people, the Pyrenean Sheepdog had never until now attracted the attention of dog lovers. Specialised literature about it is extremely poor.

Those authors who have written about it, moreover, have done so very superficially and seem to have lacked sufficient documentation.

In 1893, at a conference on sheepdogs at the National Society of Acclimatisation, P. Mégnin gave a description of the Pyrenean Sheepdog under the classification of French Sheepdogs. Four years later the Count of Bylandt, in the first edition of his *Breeds of Dogs*, gave a standard, drawn up by him, of the Pyrenean Sheepdog. There we see a dog described as having fairly long, bushy hair, with a slightly domed skull, long muzzle, small ears, eyes sometimes wall-eyed and a fairly long body.

That is the only accurate part of the description. For the rest, the errors are manifest and lead one to believe that the author spoke of this dog from hearsay only.

Joubert speaks of a dog whose gait was marked by its walking on the soles of its feet, with long, fine, silky hair ... A dog which is faithful, intelligent and submissive, a marvellous assistant to the Pyrenean herdsman.

Much later, P. Mégnin, whose cynological documentation is always interesting to consult, quotes an even more fantastic description by Brehm, who speaks of a dog "with hair which is almost stiff, curly in a young dog, and which is white with black patches. It is tall, lean and well-muscled; toes well spread out; large, well developed head; ears fairly pointed and drooping, long square muzzle and large, protruding blue eyes showing intelligence, gentleness and fearlessness."

And P. Mégnin, who is inclined to recognise in this description the descendant of the Mastiff of Gaston Phoebus (a 14th century Comte de Foix) adds the following corrections: "The Pyrenean Sheepdog is a griffon whose head has less hair; it has only a few long hairs on the eyebrows, but it does not have a pronounced moustache or beard. It is on the hind quarters that the hair has accumulated, where it has copious trousers and a thick covering on the thighs; the legs are almost bare. The feet are very spread out and recall the paw of a bear. The ears also are erect instead of lying flat. As for the colour, this is not white with large black patches, but silver grey with the said black patches, with or without a flame colour on the paws, a colour which is commonly called 'danoisé' (Danish). The eyes are frequently wall-eyed, that is to say with a bright blue iris."

More recently one can point to several articles which have appeared at long intervals in the specialised press, whose authors deal only very superficially with the dog in which we are interested.

In fact it is by word of mouth that the most complete documentation of the Pyrenean Sheepdog comes to us ... by the mountain firesides during the winter evenings, sons often repeat what their fathers have told them, and traditions, like customs, go back a long way ...

Some people are surprised at not being able to find

a complete uniformity of type in these dogs in the Pyrenees. As if, in fact, a comparable diversity of sheepdog types did not exist more or less throughout France! ... So that one would wish to report on the history of the different breeds of sheepdog before the zootechnical idea intervened in their selection; one can always see a basic type there, the original type from which the numerous varieties evolved, depending on the breeding and the environment.

It is the same in the Pyrenees as elsewhere, and no more nor less than elsewhere, and although a difference must be noted in the Pyrenean region, it certainly rests not so much upon morphological differences in the varieties of its dogs as upon their distribution among the mountain zones.

This can be explained when one bears in mind the difficulties of communication, and as a result the lack of contact that once existed between the Pyrenean valleys. In each region, isolated from its neighbours, one variety, or rather one family of dogs tended to singularise and assert itself. In time, as a result of heavy inbreeding, secondary features tended to become exaggerated and were added to the range of characteristics.

This fact has been the basis of certain opinions which, after too superficial an examination and a hasty generalisation, inferred the existence of several types of Pyrenean Sheepdogs.

In the absence of any formal documentation it was a question of bringing to light the type which, by its ethnic qualities, asserted itself as the nearest to the original and the best adapted to its surroundings. There was therefore reason to take account of physical and temperamental characteristics, the qualities and faults of the dog, its inherited factors, and its employment.

The oldest evidence confirming its hereditary qualities as a working dog, and the fact that it was a unique type, bearing no resemblance to other sheepdog breeds, either French or foreign, permit us to conclude that it is an indigenous type ...

On 18th March, 1923, we wrote in the canine magazine *L'Eleveur (The Breeder)*:

> This dog, whose long existence in the Pyrenees has been proved to us by evidence going back more than a century and a half, seems to be the true indigenous type.

In fact it presents itself as a sheepdog exhibiting a maximum of nervous energy within a minimum of height and weight. A dense fleece, straight or gently waving, mostly fawn or grey, and of a texture midway between goats' hair and sheep's wool, conceals an eminently lean skeleton. The neck, well set off from the shoulders, carries a rather fine head, characterised by a fairly short, wedge shaped muzzle; ears placed high on a skull which is almost flat and only fairly developed; with very expressive, chestnut coloured eyes, which are both mischievous and cautious. The mucous membranes are black, or well pigmented, whatever the colour of the coat. The body is rather long in relation to its height, but always compact. The chest, which is well developed in depth, descends to the level of the elbow, rarely lower. The foot is narrow, of a slightly accentuated oval shape; the hocks often rather close, especially in dogs born and bred in the mountains.

54

This dog, just as it is, represents a type perfectly adapted to its surroundings: a low centre of gravity, the result of its reduced height, assures it of a maximum of stability on the steep slopes. Its narrow foot, with a thin sole, holds onto the rocks like the rope soles of our canvas shoes. Its hocks, which follow a gentle deviation from the line of its hindquarters, are necessary for climbing up the slopes. (Try walking in the mountains with your toes turned in!)

The texture of its coat, woolly underneath and coarser on top, affords protection against violent downpours and the low temperatures. Its matchless nervous energy enables it to carry out its harsh job without faltering. Its small size allows its master to feed it parsimoniously. (How could it be otherwise with men who, for themselves, receive just the basic weekly food rations!)

Our mountain shepherds know quite well that for all these reasons they should choose a small dog. Besides, they can also see another advantage: the sheep, a good natured animal, has no need of a mastiff to drive it. If its size allows it to endure the fairly energetic pushing of a small dog, there is no need of a taller dog. If a large dog collides with a sheep, the result is probably disastrous, and something always to be dreaded in the mountains, where the slightest consequence can be a dislocated shoulder or a broken foot.

Small size, lightness of frame, well developed muscles, the nature of its coat; the Pyrenean Sheepdog needs all these to carry out his job high up in the mountains. Even his temperament, basically distrustful, and therefore vigilant, is useful to him. To see him at work it is difficult to imagine a temperament more suited to its purpose, or a physique more apt for its functions.

As for temperament, we are in the presence of a dog of a fairly independent nature, whose distrustfulness is the basis of his character. Not pampered very much, brought up to be hardy, he is generally unapproachable by strangers. He shows a certain amount of caution towards familiar people at home. There is one thing, however, which will make him forget his reserve: when the shrill whistle of the shepherd tells him that it is time for action.

Immediately he takes up his role. With a remarkable keenness for work, however young he is, he is captivated, literally possessed by his task! ... Attentive and silent, he darts effortlessly, with an easy and gentle movement around the long procession of animals. Alert to push a straggler with a nudge of his nose, to make one that has detached itself from the rest return to the ranks, to cross in front of the flock to make it go in the required direction, his whole wiry body is extended in rapid action.

But the admirable intelligence which he has for his task, knows how to check his untirable activity at the required moment. If faced with a dangerous crossing, he knows how to put a brake on his irrepressible energy, and when required, uses his skill to lead the animals one by one to a place of safety.

He excels himself in looking for a lost animal. What if a sheep is missing when they are counted? At the first command he will leave, going a long way ahead of the shepherd, searching every corner of the mountain, not leaving a corner unexplored, and using both the impulsion of a very dependable instinct and the resources of a rare intelligence.

It must be added that the Pyrenean Sheepdog is brave. I have rarely seen one of them refusing to fight something larger and taller than himself. Moreover, being generally fairly pugnacious, he is the challenger. A nimble athlete, he enters into few clinches, but proceeds by a succession of skilful dodges, and spirited and unforeseen attacks, during which a precise bite marks the adversary.

Many reasons serve as an argument in favour of those who direct their efforts towards the fixation and development of the breed. The anatomical reason, and we have explained how this dog was admirably suited to his environment – reasons of utilisation: we find him used particularly in the central region, the most mountainous area and most densely populated with flocks – reason of heredity: his resemblance to his remote ancestors is very marked by his qualities as a sheepdog –

aesthetic reasons: it is difficult to find an animal which is more appealing and more charming.

Is this not ample justification for the affection for the Pyrenean Sheepdog shown by those who know him, and even more by those who use him? ...

Equally qualified to be a working dog and a pet, his prime and inherent purpose remains, with just reason, in the eyes of the Réunion des Amateurs de Chiens Pyrénéens, the directive and the basis for his breeding. It is with this in mind that, in awarding its annual cup, it imposes on the Pyrenean Sheepdog the compulsory condition of taking part in sheepdog trials. It also thinks – and we have seen this happen to other sheepdog breeds – that the day when the Pyrenean Sheepdog is no longer a working dog, it will lose the greatest part of its personality. If working trials do not enter into breeding, breeders go more and more astray and the breed loses the fundamental qualities of the original type, which practical requirements used to maintain in a satisfactory state.

We echo the conclusions of a distinguished president of one of the sheepdog clubs:

> It is certain that one would not be able to take away from the sheepdog, the functions of a working dog which he has fulfilled for thousands of years, without running to a degeneration of type ... Without work there is no salvation. This must be, in an energetic form, the credo of the sheepdog enthusiast. Training, practical utilisation, in one word, work; is inseparable from rational breeding.

It remains well understood that we are speaking here only of 'outdoor' work. We do not place any value in competitions in the ring, where these dogs shine 'mechanically', whereas the true working dog could not show its full worth there. How could it be otherwise, with a dog whose fundamental characteristics are based on using its own initiative, and adapting to circumstances – the reverse, in fact, of that which is required of ... circus animals.

With the Pyrenean Sheepdog all classicism is excluded

from his work. He does not have a clearly defined purpose. He is a sheepdog to the core, and that is sufficient for all his tasks. With him there is no recognised division of work, and we have seen him accomplish feats which were quite disparate.

If he adapts easily to working with cattle, he is no less the ideal dog for sheep. His inherent quality is such that he works instinctively from a very young age, even without the help of an older one to teach him.

He has a tendency to know only one master, to whom he remains loyally attached, and although he is generally extremely sensitive, he will endure the harshest treatment from his master without resisting, being dominated above all by the love of his work . . . – How few men have the sense of duty developed to such a degree! –

Quite recently we have had a moving example of a little Pyrenean Sheepdog who was killed by a bear while courageously defending his flock in the absence of his master.

Previously unknown to most people, it needed the great turmoil of 1914 to bring the Pyrenean Sheepdog out of the shadows. Recruited with a zeal that was disastrous for the future of the breed, and which can be excused only by the circumstances, the brave animals fell in large numbers in the line of fire. Much appreciated as a communication dog, one could justifiably say that no other French breed has paid such a large ransom of blood, and that is a claim for which there is cause to be grateful.

This greatly diminished stock reconstituted itself slowly after the war. In the hands of peasants and mountain shepherds, who bothered little about the question of type, breeding lacked any reasonable selection. As a result, specimens approaching the ideal type were rare. However, those who are interested in breeding the Pyrenean Sheepdog know that disagreeable surprises are rare with it, and that breeding stock of the same morphological type produce, with sufficient constancy, subjects which are identical to themselves.

Our sheepdog is not exposed to those unforeseen eclipses, not only of type but also of working qualities, which indicate in others a fairly obscure pastoral origin. His constancy in inheriting physical and temperamental qualities, and his inherent strength is to us fresh proof of the orthodoxy of type which we are once more seeking in the Pyrenean Sheepdog.

Without claiming to see it spread out from one end of the mountain chain to the other in uniform abundance, one can at any rate find it there again, spreading from the Bearnese Pyrenees as far as the Black Mountain. One could almost say that it follows the area of dispersion of the Pyrenean breed of sheep, and that, like the sheep, it undergoes modifications which are more marked the further away it is from the cradle of the Breed, which remains the centre of the chain, the pastoral region par excellence.

After this insight into the Pyrenean Sheepdog it is, without doubt, good to show briefly the official efforts which have been produced on its behalf.

Immediately after the war, a small group of devotees assembled at Pau to form a club which, contrary to custom and to all logic, and without prior consultation with the breeders, drew up a standard for the long-haired Pyrenean Sheepdog which, in October 1921, it presented for confirmation by the Central Society for the Improvement of Breeds of Dog in Fance. This small group also gave a very succinct description of a dog which it designated under the name of smooth-faced Pyrenean Sheepdog.

This rather inaccurate work which was submitted to a meeting of breeders and devotees of Pyrenean Sheep-dogs at Tarbes on 11th February, 1923, necessitated fairly numerous adjustments. As for the standard relating to the smooth-faced sheepdog, this did not seem to interest the devotees who were assembled at that time.

Resulting from various meetings where everyone showed an equal desire to do good, which was justified by the fellow feeling that the Pyrenean Sheepdog inspired in them, the Réunion des Amateurs de Chiens Pyrénéens was founded in July 1923, which resolved to take some definite action about the Pyrenean Sheepdog standard.

At its General Assembly on the 21st January, 1925, the French Sheepdog Club sanctioned the efforts produced on behalf of the Pyrenean Sheepdogs, admitted them "as French sheepdogs recognised by the Club" and for the first time, in March 1926, they were admitted to the General Agricultural Show in Paris together with the breeds from Beauce and Brie.

We give below a copy of the standard of the Pyrenean Sheepdog endorsed by the Central Society for the Improvement of Breeds of Dogs in France. We will follow it with the short description officially adopted for the smooth-faced sheepdog.

Personally, we cannot see any objection to the smooth-faced, short-haired type, or at least semi-long, having official recognition. There is a Scottish sheepdog with long hair and another with short hair; Belgian sheepdogs with long hair and another with short rough hair.

It is undeniable that the smooth-faced type exists, but it is difficult to see in this dog anything other than the product of a cross between the indigenous Pyrenean type and the dogs of the sub-Pyrenean regions, and we wrote on the subject in the magazine L'Eleveur, which we mentioned previously:

> There exist in the sub-Pyrenean region, and particularly in Béarn, Bigorre and le Bassin de l'Adour a large number of sheepdogs. Their proximity of habitat and the movement of certain Pyrenean flocks which the dogs accompany are such that there are inevitably unions between them and their mountain brothers. It generally resulted in a dog with longer legs, medium length hair on the body, almost smooth on the head and legs, whose skull, rather more developed, nevertheless recalls by its shape that of the pure mountain type. Moreover, these dogs are much appreciated by the horse dealers and cattle drovers who travel around the fairs in the region.

To finish with the question of the Pyrenean Sheepdog, we would add that formerly one could find a variety of dogs in these regions, which are said to have come from

St-Béat, but which have almost completely disappeared today, and which were of a completely different type and showed a marked resemblance to the Old English Sheepdog. We haven't been able to obtain any information on their ancestry, but if by sharing the same habitat, they have a right to the title of Pyreneans, it is doubtful that their origin would confirm it to be so. From their small number and the confined radius of their habitat, it seems that such dogs should be considered as the last examples of a family which lived sporadically in the Central Pyrenees.

We mention it for the record ... Also for the record, we would point out that in Spain there is a sheepdog which looks very much like our Pyrenean Sheepdog. It is the Gos D'Atura, a Catalonian sheepdog. Here is the description which P. Mégnin gave us:

> Domed head, broad at the base, skull divided at the first third of the frontal part, occipital bone very pronounced; nose straight and in the shape of a truncated cone, lips tight, strong jaws, black mucous membranes, lips and palate; eyelids bordered with black, ears placed high, coming to a point, covered in long hair and lying close to the head, but generally they are cropped.
>
> Neck solid but short, well developed chest; sides gently curved; back horizontal, loins wide and rather short, rump raised a little, abdomen slightly tucked up; tail well set on, sometimes low, whole or docked, a maximum of 10 cm. Sloping shoulders, withers falling away, oval feet, nails and pads black, dewclaws. Coat straight or a little wavy around the paws and at the extremities; much longer on the rest of the body and coarser, almost like hair on the spine and rump. Hair colour a mixture of black and white giving a more or less dark greyish tone.
>
> Height from 0.45m to 0.50m for males; 0.43 – 0.48m for females.

Standard Of
The Pyrenean Sheepdog

General Appearance
A dog which is small in height and weight has an enormous amount of nervous energy. Characteristically always on guard, a mischievous and distrustful expression, combined with great liveliness of movement give this dog a characteristic look that has no other equal.

Faults Heavy dog without liveliness; thick muscles; ordinary expression; vicious look; trot which is short or piked.

Height
Males: 0.40 to 0.48 m (15½ – 19 in)
Females: 0.38 to 0.46 m (15 – 18 in)
A tolerance of 2 cm more is permitted in perfectly typical animals.

Elimination Height outside the limits.

Head

Fairly developed skull which is almost flat, with a central furrow showing slightly and which curves harmoniously at the sides and carries a barely pronounced occiputal projection. The front part is joined by a gently slope to the muzzle, and the crack in the nose is not apparent. In its general form the head is triangular and recalls that of a brown bear.

Faults Pointed skull; arched front; head too short, too long or too narrow; marked break in the nose; too much hair, especially when it covers the eyes.

Muzzle

Straight and rather short, letting the skull predominate on the face, slender without exaggeration and wedge shaped. The lips, which are not very thick, cover the lower jaw completely and do not show any apparent

commissure. The mucous membranes of the lips and palate are black or strongly marked with black. The nose is black. The hair on the muzzle should be as explained below under the description of the hair.

Faults Square or rectangular muzzle; muzzle too long or too short; lack of pigmentation; too much hair, hiding the eyes (see 'hair' below)

Elimination Nose not absolutely black.

Eyes

Thin eyelids bordered with black, whatever the colour of the coat, encasing expressive eyes, which are wide open and dark brown in colour. They must not be prominent nor too sunken. Eyes with a bright blue iris or speckled with bright blue are permitted in dogs with a harlequin or slate grey coat, where they are almost always a characteristic.

Faults Eyes too small, too round, pale or with a haggard expression. Lack of pigmentation on eyelids.

Elimination Eyes with a bright blue iris in dogs other than harlequin or slate grey. Scabby eyelids.

Teeth

The teeth are strong and there should be a complete set of teeth. The teeth of the top jaw cover those of the lower jaw while remaining in contact with them (Fig. no. 4). A scissor bite is permissible (Fig. no. 3).

Elimination Projecting lower jaw (Fig. no. 2) or upper jaw.

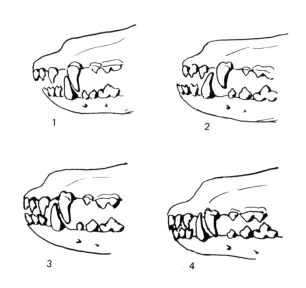

Ears

The ears should be fairly short, moderately wide at the base and placed not too close to each other on top of the head, nor too wide apart on each side of the head. They are generally cropped and well carried but those not cropped, if they are well placed, are not considered as a fault. A naturally upright ear does not exist without cross breeding. In dogs of equal merit, the dog with cropped ears which are well placed is preferred to the dog without cropped ears.

Faults Ears too low, badly carried.

Elimination Naturally upright ears.

Well-carried natural ears
Small ears   Well-formed
              2/3 upright
              1/3 turned over

Badly-carried ears
Ears too long
and heavy

Cropping

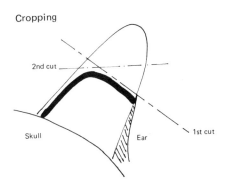

2nd cut

Skull   Ear   1st cut

Neck
Rather long, fairly well muscled, well set off from the shoulders.

Faults Neck and shoulders badly joined, neck thin or weak, set into the shoulders or too long.

Shoulders
Fairly long, medium angulation; the top of the shoulders are clearly higher than the line of the back.

Faults Shoulders too straight or too short.

Body
The framework is lean. The back fairly long, although straight; the loins short and gently arched. It also seems that the dog's coat is often more abundant on the hindquarters and the rump. The rump is rather short and fairly oblique, the flank hardly slopes, the sides are gently rounded. The chest, of medium development, falls to the level of the elbow, rarely lower.

Faults Impression of heaviness, Square dog. Horizontal back. Arched back.

Tail

Well fringed, not very long, attached rather low and with a crook at the tip. When alert, the tail must not go beyond the line of the back. Many specimens are docked. Some have a rudimentary tail which has never been shortened.

Faults Tail badly carried or without a crook at the tip.

Forelegs

Lean, sinewy, fringed with hair, with the pastern joint well revealed.

Faults Double dewclaws. Not perpendicular.

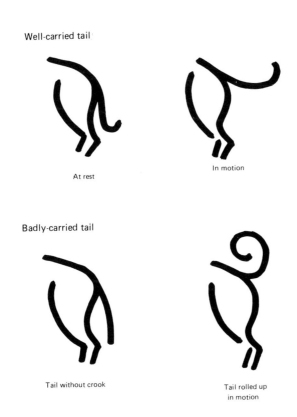

Well-carried tail

At rest

In motion

Badly-carried tail

Tail without crook

Tail rolled up
in motion

Hindquarters

The thighs are strong and do not extend downwards very much. The hocks are lean, placed low, are well bent, and are often rather close, mainly in dogs born and bred in the mountains. The angulations are fairly acute. Dogs with medium length hair have no fringes on their limbs.

The hind legs may or may not have single or double dewclaws. Dewclaws being an ancient characteristic of sheepdog breeds, those dogs with dewclaws are preferred.

Faults Straight stifles. Lack of flexibility in the joints.

Feet

Lean, fairly flat, of an accentuated oval shape. The sole is dark. The nails, small but hard, are concealed by hair which grows under the foot between the pads.

Faults Thick cat-like feet, long white nails.

Skin

Delicate, often marbled with dark patches the same colour as the coat.

Hair

Hair long or medium length, but always plentiful. Almost straight or gently waved, thicker and more woolly on the thighs and rump. The texture is a cross between the hair of a goat and the wool of a sheep. The muzzle has hair which is fairly short and on the moustache and beard, and at the sides as well as on the cheeks, the hair is brushed back 'windswept' from front to back.

The eyes should be clearly apparent and not concealed by the fur.

Faults Too much hair on the head, especially when it conceals the eyes, and on the muzzle when it takes on the appearance of a griffon's moustache. Bad texture. Curly and frizzy.

Coat

Fawn, more or less dark, with or without a mixture of black hairs, and sometimes a few white hairs on the chest and on the paws; grey, more or less light, often with white on the head, chest and paws; various shades of harlequin.

Black coats, or black marked with white, are not very prevalent. Coats of a pure colour are preferred.

Faults Too many white patches and patches which are too large. Black coat with flame on the head and legs (red socks).

Elimination for Males *Monorchidism* or *cryptorchidism*, i.e. only one testicle or none at all.

Gait

At a walking pace the Pyrenean Sheepdog has, due to his conformation, a fairly short stride; ambling is not a penalty, but it is a gait used mainly by dogs at work, with the object of lengthening the stride to follow the rhythm of the sheep, or used at the end of the day when tiredness makes itself felt, and which has no purpose in a show ring.

The trot, a gait preferred by our little sheepdog, should be free, and vigorous. At a jog-trot the head is carried fairly high; at an extended trot the head is in line with the back; the feet are never lifted very much, and the gait is flowing, it scrapes the floor.

The correct gait, which is pleasing to the eye, is due to the harmony of the shoulder-foreleg angulations.

Scale Of Points

Skull and muzzle (lips, nose)	15
Eyes	10
Ears	5
Neck, back, loins, tail	15
Shoulders, chest, sides	10
Legs and feet	15
Skin, colour, pigmentation	10
General appearance (expression, height, gait)	20
	100

It would seem to be useful for us to make a few comments on the standard given above.

It is noted that the head of the Pyrenean Sheepdog in its general shape resembles that of a brown bear. (That is a point which it is good to insist upon since the skull is the touchstone, to some extent it is a signature of the breed). We cannot find this skull, which is almost flat and fairly developed, in any other sheepdog breed. It is quite special to the Pyrenean Sheepdog.

Although it is true that this dog has, by its skull and muzzle, a certain resemblance to the brown bear, it would be puerile, as some people have a tendency to do, to try to find points throughout for comparison between the anatomy of the Pyrenean Sheepdog and that of the bear family. If our sheepdogs had the topline of a bear, they would have what, in canine slang, one calls a carp back, a defective construction in any canine species, to whatever breed it belongs. Nor could they have an exaggerated bend of the hocks or the gait of a bear. It is superfluous to dwell upon a similar absurdity which imposes on an animal which walks on its toes, the gait of an animal which walks on the soles of its feet! ...

And this leads us to say a word about gait. Perhaps the standard should have dwelt upon this point and indicated its importance. Certain dogs have a springy movement, 'piked', which is unpleasant to the eye, usually the result of anatomical imperfections, and particularly lack of angulation in the hindquarters. This gait should be regarded as improper, whatever the other qualities of the dog, and is in complete contrast to the smooth flowing gait of a working dog, of a dog which trots from the shoulder.

At intervals some dogs adopt an ambling gait. We are not unaware of the controversy which has recently brought up the question of ambling in the Pyrenean Sheepdog. Some have seen it as the result of imbalance between the fore-quarters and the hind-quarters. We do not think so. Observation has proved to us that such a gait springs from adaptation. The flocks of sheep generally stroll along at such a pace that a slightly taller dog passes them when trotting but cannot keep up with them at walking pace. He therefore has a tendency, especially on the road, to adopt this ambling gait, this mixed gait which is faster than walking, slower than a trot, which allows him to keep up with the flock. With their smaller strides, the small dogs do not need it to keep pace on the trot with the flock . . .

The standard recommends a preference for dogs with accentuated pigmentation . . . That is a biological trait on which it is superfluous to insist. In this connection it is as well to note that the pigmentation of the mucous membranes in dogs with fawn coats is almost more accentuated than that of the greys and blacks. This tends to contradict the general opinion that the pigmentation of the mucous membranes is the natural consequence of the shade of the coat, in which case wall eyes, which are almost exclusively the lot of grey or harlequin dogs, should be found in dogs with light coats . . . This would seem to be nothing other than a phenomenon of irregular pigmentation.

In their youth, our sheepdog puppies have drooping ears and, left to themselves, the ears of the adult dog are never raised. The practice of cropping is fairly widespread in the mountains. The shepherds generally do it with a knife, with a dexterity that many veterinary surgeons would envy. They take care not to damage the heel of the ear, whose lower part remains intact. The top part of the ear only is sectioned at an acute angle above the horizontal. Cropping is perhaps more or less standard and gives a very pleasing expression to the face, while not stripping the shell of the ear in too unsightly a manner.

A naturally upright ear exists in rare specimens. It is always a sign of cross breeding . . . The German Shepherd Dog has been up to his tricks again here to the great detriment of the breed, for it is extremely rare for dogs carrying this blood to wish to work with a flock.

The question of the hair is equally important, but having been submitted to many external causes capable of altering the length, the standard allows both long and medium length hair. Whatever the length of their hair, the dogs are otherwise identical in respect of their anatomy and general character. Those with medium length hair have no fringes on the hindquarters, but still keep their thick trousers. The hair on the muzzle and face is short.

Changes of lifestyle and environment are often the cause of noticeable modification in the coat, not only from the point of view of its abundance, but also of its quality. It becomes duller, drier and loses that special quality due to the freshness of the mountain air.

It is not necessary to say that if the Pyrenean Sheepdog needs a rump which is short and a little oblique, yet solid, it is to be strong enough to support a fairly long, and therefore supple, back which lends itself easily to the many different movements required in the mountains.

The development of the chest, generally satisfactory in breadth, is a little faulty in depth. I understand that some people will object that there is incompatibility between the lack of chest and the irrepressible activity shown by our Pyrenean Sheepdogs. We reply that the spirometer has proved that animals with an impressive thoracic perimeter do not have the largest respiratory capacities, but those with a long thorax do. And now there are facts which demonstrate that if our sheepdogs work with an untirable ardour, they do so because of their nervous energy, their admirable vitality and their grit.

With regard to height, the standard indicates limits of 38 and 50 cm. Although we have seen dogs measuring 36 cm managing perfectly with the flock, it would seem that it was a wise move to limit the minimum height to 38 cm. All the prize winners at official shows from 1920 to 1927 were carefully measured by us, and were within the height limits indicated in the standard. The maximum height, realised once only, was 49 cm.

There was therefore no reason at all to fix the maximum height of this dog at 55 cm, as did the original and rather imprecise standard. Observation proves, moreover, that the shorter dogs are generally the better type, wthout doubt because their ancestry was free from any crossing with the larger dogs which exist in the sub-Pyrenean region.

The question of dewclaws has caused a lot of ink to

flow elsewhere and for other working breeds. It seems to have been resolved for the best here. It is difficult to maintain that the presence of supplementary toes has any use today. Those who favour the dewclaw, which others call a spur, will have it that sometimes the dog uses it as a brake on steep slopes.

To tell the truth, we have never noticed that the dewclaw acts as a brake, even on the loosest ground. It is only in snow that we have been able to distinguish the track made by the dewclaw, when it exists as an actual toe and is not reduced to the state of an atrophied organ being held onto the leg by a small piece of skin only ... However, the standard considers very rightly, and we can only approve, that as the dewclaw is a characteristic of sheepdog breeds, specimens with dewclaws should be preferred.

The tail may be long, naturally short or docked. We will point out, without comment, a barbarous practice sometimes used: some shepherds, after dividing the puppies' tail with their nails, remove them by twisting them off!

Standard Of The Smooth-Faced Pyrenean Sheepdog

This dog, which is less nervous and more malleable than the long-hair sheepdog, and less cautious towards strangers, nevertheless shows much gaiety and spirit.

On the whole it possesses the same characteristics as the long-haired sheepdog. It differs in that it has a slightly longer muzzle. Its head is covered with short, fine hair (hence smooth-faced), the hair on the body is of medium length or shorter, reaching its greatest length of 6 to 7 cm on the neck and withers, and 4 to 5 cm on the mid-line of the back.

The legs are smooth-haired with a light fringe of hair on the front legs and trousers on the back legs. The tail may be long with a crook at the tip, or docked. Many specimens have a short tail at birth. The foot is both more compact and more arched than that of the long-haired Pyrenean Sheepdog.

Keeping the same proportions, the body is a little shorter than that of the long-haired Pyrenean Sheepdog.

Permitted coat colours are black, harlequin, brindle, various shades of fawn with or without a mixture of black hairs and sometimes a few white markings. Grey coats are not very common.

The height of the smooth-faced sheepdog varies from 0.40 m to 0.54 m (15½ – 21 in) for males and from 0.40 m to 0.52 m (15½ – 20½ in) for females.

Faults and eliminations are the same as those indicated for the long-haired variety.

We have done our best to leave to those who trouble to read these lines, a picture as accurate as possible of our Pyrenean dogs. The fancier should not forget that knowledge of a breed is quite a different thing from the mere study of its standard, which is only the concrete result of a series of descriptive abstractions.

The study of the standard alone, without a long and constant acquaintance with the breed, is nothing. Whatever the accuracy of a description, it will have little or no effect in developing those imponderables which result in 'an eye for a dog', without which all judgement is worthless. This is where, above all, the qualities of temperament and the psychology of the breed come in, which are resonsible for maintaining it in its proper place.

With both the Mountain Dog and the Pyrenean Sheepdog, being issues of a common environment and being imprinted with identical atavisms, where the essential qualities of work predominate, there should be numerous similarities, upon which the confines of a book do not allow us to elaborate. In the first place they are endowed with the same vigilance, the same high sense of duty, the same attachment for the object of their concern.

At the time of writing these lines, one of our sheepdog bitches is lying beside us. Her expressive eyes, tawny and black, follow each of our movements with untirable attention. Let an unexpected movement disturb her quietude, and she will be on her feet in a flash, on guard against any surprise.

I never grow tired of admiring this eternal 'on guard', the magnificent predominance of an instinct which is ready for any eventuality, the ancestral heritage of creatures who have always lived at liberty in the mountains away from the regulated ways of the civilised animal.

The mountains? It is to them that our dogs owe their charm and their personality. And in these few lines, where we have tried to show them as they are, we hope will be found not only a proof of their profound affection, but also, indirectly, a testimony of unfailing attachment to the setting in which they live, to the native land so dear to the heart of every mountain dweller. Majestic giants and alert sheepdogs, born like us under its sky, they have breathed its breezes, they have drunk from its torrents, they hold within themselves something of its remote untamed charm, and when distance deprives us of the great joy of our native environment, we bend towards their affectionate heads and seek to find once again, in the light of their eyes, the friendly profile of the distant mountains.

It would seem that we should finish on these words, as poetic as they are eulogistic and moving. I am telling nothing new when I say that one does not tire of speaking about something that one loves.

We cannot resist the pleasure of telling you about the appraisal of a professional man, M. Ph Defrance, a former pupil of the Ecole de Rambouillet, who in June 1948 wrote in *Chiens et Vénerie (Dogs and Hunting)*:

> The reflexes of the Pyrenean Sheepdog are incomparable and superior to those of all the other sheepdog breeds; his obedience and his fidelity are remarkable. His initiative, his judgement and his memory never fail him when he is put to the test. His courage results from his obduracy to suffering (sometimes insufficient food in the mountains). When the bitches have the necessary nutritive elements in their rations, they are nothing less than excellent milkers.
>
> If this dog has a fault, it is his lack of size; but who would not recognise that at the present time, it is an advantage from the point of view of feeding. It is also, thanks to the small space that it occupies, the ideal guardian of the motor car.
>
> Seen as a sheepdog, the little Pyrenean is irreplaceable in the mountains. On the plain, nothing is too keen to escape his eye.

The little Pyrenean, a guard dog and police dog? Certainly. He is very vicious when he attacks, and very easy to train for all the tests. It is quite evident that he would not break any world records for negotiating obstacles, but no other dog of comparable height is capable of such ease. To give an example, my male, who measured 45 cm at the shoulders and had an injury to his front paw, without any special training jumped over a pasture enclosure with barbed wire on top, a sheep hurdle and a six foot high stone wall, and I am certain that Pyrenean Sheepdogs can jump more than two metres (6 ft 6 in).

At this height, they can already render an appreciable service, and can participate in competitions in the ring.

For guarding flats and children the little Pyrenean, which is by nature a very clean animal, is simply ideal.

This breed, which has not been made popular by anybody famous, is bound to become so only through its many qualities to the extent to which they are made known, and that is the duty of the breeders.

Take a little Pyrenean for a walk, no matter where, and you will hear everyone say, "Oh, what a lovely dog! What expressive eyes! What breed is it? One doesn't see them very much! I would love to have one like that! etc!" In some way this is a resumé of what I have just told you.

And in my turn, having personally been both a sheep breeder and a Pyrenean Sheepdog breeder, I have had occasion to speak of them in the January 1966 issue of *La Vie des Bêtes (Animal Life)*, and to say in particular,

> It is not excessive to claim that this little dog has a human character. Whatever the circumstances, whatever his work, whatever his role, he knows how to rise to his task.

And in the same issue of January 1966 I was able to give examples of this instinct for work:

An incorruptible guardian, one can trust him to guard anything. On several occasions I have seen our dogs, to whom the shepherdess, obliged to go away, had left the care not only of the flock but also of her deck-chair and knitting, warn her furiously at the approach of a stranger. One can rely upon them. Let me give an anecdote showing their initiative.

During the winter, to fatten the young ones, we used to drive the lambs into a special pen to give them a supplementary ration. The lambs learnt very fast and the manoevre was easy.

Willy was always there, sitting close to the door; one could have sworn that she was counting the lambs on their way in. One day, as soon as they finished filing out, she went as usual to visit the pen where the little ones had come from, and immediately returned, frantic to find the shepherdess, trying to make her understand that she had to come and look. Seeing her indifference, she pulled at the hem of her apron. By chance I was there and accompanied the shepherdess, who wanted to find out what the trouble was. In the pen was found a lamb wedged behind a rack, and out of breath from struggling. *Willy* licked the head of the little animal for more than five minutes to comfort it, and went with it to find its mother again.

Like M. Defrance, I have tested, without researching, the tracking abilities of my old *Bichou* (a son of *Willy*) who was my inseparable companion for ten years – one of the most intelligent dogs I have ever had – who when once left at home for various reasons, came to fetch me some kilometers away, following my trail step by step across the fields at a very rapid pace, proving to me the point to which they were able to make themselves useful during the 1914–18 war. Guarding the car, he would not let it be approached by anyone without barking furiously, ready to jump at anyone who touched it.

This dog acclimatises himself in any country. Very playful and very gay, he is the joy of the family. The friends of those who own one, on seeing him at his various tasks, quickly wish in their turn to adopt this rustic companion, with an excellent temperament and so faithful, and whose cleanliness cannot be equalled.

Another anecdote:

It reminds me of having read in the *Vie Canine* (No. 40) under the name of Madame Mad Vilette, a sensational anecdote which made her ask this question:

Does a dog sense danger?

Professor L, a radiologist, was the owner of a little Pyrenean Sheepdog which never left him.

In the calm of his office-library one evening, Professor L, was at his work. His dog *Ami* was stretched out full length on the carpet and slept soundly. The silence was deep, the hour peaceful.

Suddenly *Ami* was dragged from his slumber – 'dragged' is the exact word, the word which suits perfectly: a dog that is sleeping deeply does not awake by himself – he opened his eyes and stood up. Worried, he went to the door, returned, went back again.

The professor carried on writing, he was completely immersed in his work; and then he noticed his dog, it was a lively animal, fidgety by nature, so he did not pay attention to *Ami*'s antics. The latter persisted, crying. "Yes, yes," said his master, with his mind on something else, "Wait a minute."

But *Ami* was irritated at not being understood. He increased his comings and goings from the desk to the door; scratched at it and then grew bold and pulled at the bottom of his master's trousers. In a rage the professor got up and went to the door – *Ami*, finally you . . . – he did not have time to finish when, tearing itself away from the wall where it had been fixed for decades, the big bookcase on the wall behind the desk fell with a crash into the middle of the room, engulfing the desk and the furniture nearby.

Very pale, the professor took his rescuer in his arms and his affection for him from then on was doubled with a profound gratitude, mixed with respect.

What explanation can be found? It could have been that certain noises, hardly perceptible by the professor absorbed in his work, awoke the dog and made him aware of the danger, as in the mountains his fellows sense avalanches. And how many other similar phenomena which are unknown to us.

Breeding

We invite our readers to refer to what we have expounded for the Pyrenean Mountain Dogs. The advice is the same, keeping everything in proportion.

As with all breeds, our little bitches have litters of very varying numbers, on average 4 – 5 puppies.

On two occasions – two different bitches – I have had litters of 7 good sized puppies. One bitch, a very good milker, raised them quite naturally by herself, right up to weaning, having begun very early (at about three weeks) to give as a supplement her own meals half digested. The other, more egotistical, never did it, and moreover revealed herself to have insufficient milk for more than four little ones. I was able to test on her, with complete satisfaction, a product which developed the milk secretion and augmented its quality.

Recently, with a young two year old bitch having her first litter, and who was a poor milker, I was able to get her to raise her four little ones, under remarkable conditions, with injections of 2 cc of this product each day for a month. At six weeks she still had almost enough milk. I am not afraid to insist on the necessity of rich and abundant food for the nursing bitches. Worm them before mating. Good food, vitamins and calcium should be given during gestation, and continued during milking. A good milker must eat at least 250 – 300 g of fresh meat each day.

She should not get thin while feeding her young. After three weeks the pups can start to lap. At one month they should be wormed to rid them of their ascarids (they all have them). The tail can be docked the day after birth, the ears at six weeks. Vaccination can be carried out at three months. Training will be the same as that already given for the large Pyreneans.

Keep your little friends near you. Let them live with you. A basket in the lobby. A box of sawdust for their needs. Fresh water constantly at their disposal.

Attend to hygiene and cleanliness every morning or every evening; as for the large dogs. Once more, pay attention to ticks. The weaning of young ones is a delicate matter. In litters, there are some greedy ones who eat twice as fast as the others. It is wise to supervise meal-times and give each one his own bowl. Those that are greedy can get indigestion and develop diarrhoea. As long as they have a little milk from their mother, this milk regulates the digestion. When it disappears, they should be given one or two tablets of lactic acid in a little milk as a preventative. If that is not sufficient, reduce the ration and consult your veterinary surgeon. As soon as the first days of weaning are over, prepare their meals with vegetable broth. Give plenty of green vegetables, 40 – 50g of raw minced meat, and rice. Give raw grated carrot as a substitute for boiled vegetables. Get your puppy used to drinking a little coffee and to eating fruit. From time to time give him grilled or boiled fish, which contains plenty of phosphate, and finally calcium and vitamins for at least six months. Above all never give food with too much broth. The food should be soft but fairly solid and always given lukewarm.

The Origins Of The Réunion Des Amateurs De Chiens Pyrénéens

At the request of a certain number of our members, I was nominated to write a historical account of our club. This historical account, which was published in three issues of *Vie Canine* in 1959 is, I think, interesting to reproduce here as a conclusion to what we have just written about our dogs. It is recognised by everyone that a breed cannot be preserved and improved unless it is taken in hand by people who are qualified and dedicated to conserve the type, at the risk of appearing severe. That is what we strive to do in following the directives and principles of those who preceded us.

Unfortunately most of the founders and moving spirits have disappeared, leaving only a few traces of their activity. I had to rely on the memory of those who knew them. I apologise in advance if there are any gaps in my information.

"The Great Pyreneans" have been known for a long time and it was, in short, the 1914–18 war which revealed our little sheepdogs. Shortly after the victory, M. Dhers expressed his thoughts thus: "In my capacity as former training officer in the Military Dog Service, it is my duty to proclaim proudly that it is the small Pyrenean Sheepdog breed that supplied the army with the most knowing, the fastest and most useful communication dogs."

In his thesis (1927) the veterinary surgeon Dr Dutrey tells us that it was immediately after the war that a little group of enthusiasts assembled at Pau to form a club which, contrary to custom and to all logic, without consultation with the breeders, drew up a standard which in 1921 it presented for the approval of the Centrale. This was a false start.

In July 1923, under the fortunate initiative and impulsion of M. Senac-Lagrange, whose competence was great and extensive, and who was its great initiator, a second meeting took place at Tarbes, where the Réunion des Amateurs de Chiens Pyrénéens (Reunion of Pyrenean Dog Enthusiasts) was founded, incorporating as its name suggests, both the large and small Pyreneans.

While the first group were making their false move in 1921, Colonel Tolet gathered together an enthusiastic and dynamic group of amateurs who were full of 'spirit' and created the French Pyrenean Sheepdog Club, whose evolution we will first of all try to follow up until its amalgamation with the R.A.C.P.

The first committee was, therefore, presided over by Colonel Tolet, with Mme Caron-Savalle and M. Pierre Poey as vice-presidents, and members who were well known personalities in the dog world, such as the Baroness de Malaret, M. Barais, Dr Ereinbert, Messrs Beruyer and Jacquin. There were 22 members, an excellent start ... And during this prosperous time between the two wars, one could see at the shows in Paris and in the provinces, some fine dogs such as those of M. Pierre Poey – *Poilu, Mouche* and *Briam* undisputably of a good type; *Gamin* from the Edeva kennel owned by Colonel Tolet; some very beautiful subjects from the de la Miche kennels owned by Madame Perdrizet; the famous stud dog *Marmot* owned by Mme Caron-Savalle; the *Baigory* of Mme Marcy, and also *L'Ami* and *Fine Mouche* belonging to M. Poey, whose photo still serves as an advertisement for the Pyrenean region, having obtained the great Diploma of Honour. Some excellent breeders like M. and Mme Sesaller exhibited a very pretty type from the *La Croix du Bouquet* kennel owned by Mme Caron.

During the occupation they were deported. Their unfortunate bitch *Itessa* could not console herself at their disappearance and died of grief. We salute their memory in passing.

In 1939 the Committee had His Majesty the Emperor of

Annam as Honorary President. Mme Guerlain replaced M. Poey as vice president.

M. and Mme Frei were secretary and treasurer, Mlle Solier publicity.

The 1939 war brought a very hard blow to the Club. Dr Ereinbert fell on the field of honour; Colonel Tolet died in 1941 on his estate at Tavers in Loiret. The Club, decapitated, lay dormant. Regrouped in 1945 by M. Frei, the presidency was offered to M. Senac-Lagrange who accepted, and a temporary committee was formed: M. Senac-Lagrange, President: M. Legendre, Vice president; Secretary/treasurer, M. Frei; Members; Mesdames Frey, Marcy, Messrs Barais, Dr Bertrand. The journal *Chiens et Venérie* which had just been created became the mouthpiece of the *French Pyrenean Sheepdog Club*. A general meeting was convened on 15th June, 1946 to elect a permanent committee. The provisional committee was maintained; the offices remained the same. The shows resumed and once again one found in the prize list at Paris representatives of the old, well-known affixes *du Canast, la Croix du Bouquet, des Loubonnieres, La Vallère, de la Miche*, of which we must salute in passing the excellent reproducer *Nérou de la Miche*, sire of numerous, very good descendants. Nor must we forget the excellent *Cascade de l'Adour* also belonging to Mme Perdrizet. Mme Marcy, having succeeded in maintaining her *Baigory* breeding during the war, and we can still find her blood-lines in today's pedigrees.

At the general meeting of 16th June 1947 approval was given to the Minutes of the Committee Meeting on 16th November 1946, and it was unanimously agreed to dissolve the French Pyrenean Sheepdog Club and to affiliate it with the R.A.C.P.

We have written previously that on the initiative of M. Senac-Lagrange the club 'Réunion des Amateurs de Chiens Pyrénéens' was founded. The articles were filed at the sub-prefecture of Argelès on 20th November 1923 and the Declaration of Constitution was published in the *Journal Officiel* of 15th December of the same year. The society's office was established at the home of M. Camazon-Mouton, 34 rue d'Argelès at Lourdes with a founder Committee made up as follows: Vice Presidents Messrs Cazenavette, Chêne, Claverie, Lassalle, Pragnères and Dr Segot.

In 1927 a yearbook published by M. Senac gives a clear picture of our grouping at that time. There seems to have been a real manifestation of 'fire', of enthusiasm, a spirit of emulation which certainly led the breeding of Pyreneans to a point that has never been equalled. The followers were spread throughout the whole of France, about one hundred in number. Breeding establishments were numerous and important in both breeds.

It is not possible for us to give a complete list, but we will give the most notable ones which have registered an affix. Lacking documents, it is difficult to follow the life of the club from day to day. We have however found a 1931 yearbook "Manual of the perfect breeder" which from its show reports indicates the 'stars' and their faults, which seem to us very interesting to list for the benefit of new breeders.

First look at the Great Pyreneans. The main kennels are:

D'Ouront belonging to M. Blanchard with 2 stud dogs and 3 bitches

Des Pyrénées belonging to M. Bordebat with 2 stud dogs and 4 bitches

De Soum belonging to M. Cazau Moutou with 3 stud dogs and 6 bitches

De Betpouey belonging to M. Lassalle with 5 stud dogs and 10 bitches

De Langladure belonging to M. Le Conte with 1 stud dog and 3 bitches

De Lutèce belonging to M. de Cessé with a breeding pair

Du Pic du Jer belonging to M. Abadie-Toulet, which is still in existence.

There are also a number of other breeders, more modest and without an affix who, for this reason, are difficult to follow, but nevertheless produced good specimens.

In 1930 M. Senac-Lagrange, who had followed very closely the evolution of the breed in almost all the shows, wrote:

Of some 200 subjects which we have examined since the war, some fifty merited serious consideration. Due to lack of space we will not continue the study of these fifty subjects.

We will mention one only, *Patou de Betpouey*, a fine and congenial dog who from 1920 to 1925 retained first place amongst those presented for showing, which is the surest indication of quality. It is from him that *Gazost de Betpouey* issued, substantial without heaviness, well coupled, supported by good limbs resting on good feet, with an expressive face and good pigmentation. In fact, *Gazost* is the ideal type of stud dog to look for. It is not necessary to point out that the male that is tolerably close to the ground is more useful than the big dog, so rarely successful, too often ungainly. Is the generality of females better than the males? The reply could be affirmative if one takes into account that, because of their sex, they more readily show this elegant style with which the males are often less endowed. Their stylishness helps to emphasise their breed-type, whatever the merits or otherwise of their conformation. *Estellou de Langladure* is a perfect example. Too small, but what a charming, unique expression. The expression of this dog seizes the observer, penetrates him, makes him sense intensely the inestimable moral courage which is the 'Pyrenean expression'. Indefinable. Impossible to describe.

In conclusion, M. Senac-Lagrange declared:

> The dog of the Pyrenees will remain himself because he is not like any other; defying all strange surroundings, he escaped the caprice of fashion.
>
> Let us pay tribute to this magnificent dog of ancestral nobility, who can assert his perpetuity without flagging during the passage of centuries.

May our present breeders think about these last remarks.

The same impetus was produced for the sheepdogs, and we have pleasure in mentioning all the best breed lines, unfortunately almost all of which have disappeared.

Always at the head, for the little dogs as for the big ones:

de Soum belonging to M. Camazou-Mouton comprising 2 breeding pairs;

Elhura belonging to Mme Berthe, 2 stud dogs and 4 bitches;

Seillan belonging to M. Chene, one breeding pair;

de Turon belonging to M. Dardignac, 4 stud dogs and 11 bitches;

Du Val d'Or belonging to M. Dhers;

du Grand Jar belonging to M. Jomini, 1 breeding pair;

de Semeac belonging to Dr Laccassagne, 1 stud dog and 2 bitches;

de l'Adour belonging to M. Lamaignère, 3 stud dogs and 7 bitches;

de Mulato belonging to M. Rosapelly, 1 stud dog and 3 bitches;

Ganast belonging to Mme Demante;

des Gaves belonging to M. Barais;

de la Grave belonging to M. Cabanne, Dr Sigot, 4 stud dogs and 7 bitches, and finally

the *Lucvielle* kennel with about 20 dogs belonging to M. Senac-Lagrange. *des Fontanettes* is the continuation of this, and dogs of these two affixes can be found at the root of many of the present good breed lines.

Each of the kennels that we have just listed had its stars.

In Paris M. Lamaignère exhibited a group of grey dogs whose type and uniformity attracted every commendation. We often find in the list of prize winners a succession of the beautiful *l'Adour* dogs. *L'Elhura* counts as its best winner at Paris, and in the provinces, *Youcki*, a small, very pleasing harlequin. Dr Sigot, an enthusiast of the Pyrenean Sheepdog, owned a very important kennel with some remarkable dogs, whose outlines were very captivating.

It would take too long to enumerate all the others.

To finish, we will mention the *du Turon* kennel belonging to M. Dardignac who showed in the rings the brightest jewel in his crown; *Nanouck* a dark grey endowed with an excellent coat, a very good frame and a very expressive head. The *Lucveille* kennel had the rare good fortune to count amongst its breeding, the champion *Berouyette*, sole and unrivalled champion of the breed, an incomparable bitch who was never beaten. In 1925 the great prize of honour of the Minister of Agriculture was awarded to her, crowning an impressive list of prizes. She had descendants worthy of her. We will end this retrospective glance with this appreciation written by the chronicler Berye in 1930:

> The main attraction of the shows was the appearance of *Champion Berouyette de Lucveille* flanked by her two daughters *Amourette* and *Calypso*. Those who saw this incomparable trio of bitches with expressive faces, a flowing gait so that the general appearance of the breed was supremely revealed, can flatter themselves at having had in front of their eyes the most beautiful success that it is possible to dream of.

We come once again to 16th June, 1947, the day after the merging of the Pyrenean Sheepdog Club of France with the Réunion des Amateurs de Chiens Pyrénéens, whose committee had now been joined by M. and Mme Frei, M. Barais, M. Boudreaux, still under the presidency of M. Senac-Lagrange. The driving force had vanished. The old kennels had in part disappeared. Others were made known, others were to appear; thanks to the Newsletters, it will be much easier for us to follow the life of the club from then on.

Amongst our sheepdogs, as immediately after the 1914 war, a movement takes form and, little by little, we see new breed lines appear at the same time as certain ones, which have lain dormant, make their reappearance.

In January 1946, M. and Mme Frei registered their *de la Pastorale* affix, which very quickly assured an important production of quality, thanks to a judicious choice of breeding stock of good origin, selected from the well known kennels *Les Loubonnières, L'Alarie, de Baigory, de Montmartel, des Fontanettes* and *du Pas de l'Ours.*

At the meeting of 24th May, 1948, M. Legendre was elected a member of the committee in place of M. Boudreaux who had resigned. The members present proceeded to examine the different questions treated in the 1948 yearbook and insisted on the most desirable presence of double dewclaws in the sheepdog. Where the large dogs were concerned, it was specified that double dewclaws were obligatory. The absence of double dewclaws on the hind legs is an **elimination**.

At the meeting at Pau on 30th April, 1949, M. Legendre had died. An amendment was made to article 7 of the statutes. The committee decided to provide for the replacement of certain of its members who had died or resigned by filling the vacancies by new nominations, to be ratified at the general meeting which followed. An amendment was also made to article 2 of the statutes. The Society's office would from now on be at the home of the Secretary/Treasurer. Article 5 was also amended: "The duration of the mandate for committee members is altered from three to five years."

The following committee members were appointed: Mmes Vigeant and Lamaz, Messrs Delattre, Cabanne and Pezet. The officers were therefore: M. Senac-Lagrange, President; Mme Frei and M. Ch Duconte, Vice-Presidents: M. Frei, Secretary/Treasurer. The other members of the committee were Mmes Senac-Lagrange, Perdrizet, Vigeant, Lamaz; Messrs Barais, Cabanne, Delattre and Pezet. The Committee agreed the conditions of appointment for judges nominated by the R.A.C.P. This year, 1949, was really the time when the activities of the club and of breeding were set on a straight course.

The Special Show at Pau on 1st May, 1949 was revived, with a rather pleasing lot of sheepdogs, 7 males and 7 females, the judging of which was entrusted to M. Duconte, of which the two lots bred by Mme Senac-Lagrange and Dr Gleizes were very noteworthy.

Concerning the large Pyreneans, as M. Delattre had made the great sacrifice of bringing his dogs, there was a large entry, all of good quality. I regret not being able to give the critique drawn up by the judge, M. Pezet, the day after the show on the 11 males and 9 females that were presented to him. The C.A.C. (Challenge Certificate) and C.A.C.I.B. were awarded, among the males, to the excellent *Sultan* owned by M. Collongue, the reserve to *Ursus de Pontoise; Roland de Soum* belonging to M. Sales and *Utlic* followed, both being marked "Excellent".

Amongst the females, the first prize went to *Mounia* owned by M. Collongue, a daughter of *Roland de Soum*. Second was *Wylione de Pontoise* owned by M. Delattre.

The medal for the best breeder was awarded to M. Delattre.

The Special Show of Sheep and Cattle Dogs in October was something of a highlight for our Pyrenean Sheepdogs: 27 (12 + 15) filed into the ring for M. Lamarque, including 11 *de la Pastorale* dogs. From the results, some of these dogs were to increase the reputation of their kennels. In the prize list for the Open Male Class, we once again find *Ubac des Fontanettes* owned by Mme Vigeant, who was to have an excellent show career.

Wip du Pas de l'Ours, whose life was short, belonged to M. Frei. In C.J.M. (Young Male), *Weg de la Pastorale* who was destined for a brilliant career and, belonging to the beginner M. Sabouraud, was at the base of the *de Fleurac* kennel. In C.O.F. (Open Bitch), *Wallis de la Pastorale* owned by Mme Frei, and *Woodie de la Pastorale* belonging to Mme de Courtillole, took away the C.A.C. and the Reserve.

In C.J.F. (Young Bitch) *Wattine de Pastorale* belonging to Mme Frei and *Willy de la Pastorale* owned by M. Sabouraud were in the first places. The 11 *de la Pastorale* dogs brilliantly carried away the breeders prize. At the end of 1949, as the journal *Chiens et Vénerie* was now being published very irregularly, it was abandoned by the Club, who decided to give information direct by duplicated bulletins; these bulletins, collected in the archives, constitute a precious source of information.

The Paris Show in 1950 was a success for the *de Pontoise* breeding for the big dogs, and for the *de la Pastorale* kennel with the small ones.

A lovely presentation at the Cauterets Special Show on 30th July of the same year. Amongst the large Pyreneans, *Sultan* owned by M. Collongue was declared to be a model of the breed. In the Sheepdogs, *Wattine de la Pastorale* belonging to Mme Frei took the cup for Best in Show.

Another special Sheepdog Show at Tarbes in October saw a large number of *Les Fontanettes* carrying away all the first prizes.

From 1951 onwards we were to see a whole list of new affixes represented at the shows, and some of the old ones continued:

De Castelviehl belonging to Mme Vigeant – *de l'Arbizon* belonging to M. Casou – *De Friminargue* belonging to M. Breton – Mme Marcy's *De Batgory* – Mme Perdrizet's *De la Miche* – M. Bourriette's *De Darrespouey* – Dr Gleizes' *Du Pas de l'Ours* – M. Largiller's *de Montmartel* – M. Ardaens' *De la Chardonière* – M. Crist's *Des Loubonnières* – Mlle Esther Rolland's *De la Caverne de l'Ours* – M. Paul Dauphin's *De Beth Ceu* – M. J. A. Sabouraud's *De Fleurac*, with *Weg and Willy de la Pastorale* – Mme la Générale Gorisse's *de Speyrous* – Mme de Courtilloles *Du Clos St Pierre* – Mme Nicolosi's *De l'Espinouse* – Mme Van Vooren's *De Bethmale* – Mme Cauvin's *De la Cusselière* – Mme Blain's *De la Roubine* – Mme Boyer's *De Gabardées* – M. Grassini's *Vaillancoeur* – Mme Morière-Bernadotte's *Du Four à Chaux* – Mme Raveau's *Du Batlaitous* – M. Aucla's *De Beaucite* – M. Dorneau's *De la Croix-Fronsac*.

We can still find some old faithfulls like *le Pas de l'Ours – Pontoise* which is flourishing – *Poeymayou* belonging to Mlle Lamazou-Betbeder – Mme Vissault's *La Cime d'Azur* – Mme Mylio Saleza's *Du Jaout* – Mlle Leger's *De Guerveur* – M. Billot's *Du Hyeron* – Mme Lanaz's *Berny Cottage* – M. Aladie Toulet's *Du Pic de Jer – Le Comté de Foix* belonging to Dr Giralt.

There were many other Pyreneans whose owners never felt it necessary to have an affix and register their dogs.

At the general meeting of 28th July, 1952 at Cauterets, the committee was re-elected and M. Ch Douillard returned.

At the committee meeting in Paris on 4th April 1954, Mme Frei the vice-president, announced the death on 17th March, 1954 of M. Senac-Lagrange, the president. M. Sabouraud was appointed to replace him on the committee. At another meeting on the following 11th July, the election of a president was held and M. Ch Duconte was elected.

At the beginning of 1955 the duplicated bulletin was abandoned and the Club news was communicated through alternate issues of *Vie Canine*, the first being that of April 1955. Mme Senac-Lagrange was elected Vice President in place of M. Duconte.

During the winter of 1955-56, M. Frei resigned from the committee, and Mme Frei also.

At the committee meeting at Auch on 10th June 1956, M. J. A. Sabouraud was nominated for the position of Secretary/Treasurer, and at the general meeting on 29th July, 1956, a vote was taken with a view to completing the committee to replace M. Barais, who had died, and M. and Mme Frei, who had resigned. M. Heid, M. Gaudry and M. Nicolosi were elected. At a committee meeting on the same day, Mme Perdrizet was elected Vice President and M. André Delattre Joint Secretary, at the request of M. J. A. Sabouraud, to help him with matters concerning the large Pyreneans. In 1957 the Powers of the Committee were renewed. This election took place at a general meeting in Paris on 10th March. Mesdames Blain and de Courtilloles were elected to complete the committee, whose officers remained the same.

Some new breeders registered their affixes. These were: Mme Delhalle's *Du pic d'Estibat* – Mme Rabouille's *le Manoir de Riquemesnil* – Mme Lebbé's *Du clos de Neiges* – Mme Lampert's *De La Franche Pierre* which got off to an excellent start – M. Follenfant's *Des Cèdres Bleus*, all of which were devoted to the breeding of the Big dogs. Mme Lafille's *du Mont-Notre-Dame* – Mme de Portalon's *Du Bosq d'Aure* – and M. Fontaine's *De la Grezette* for the Sheepdogs.

We come to 1962. Re-election of the committee of which we give a complete list here as it is "still in force as we write (1967)".

M. Charles Duconte – President
Mme Senac-Lagrange and Mme Perdrizet – Vice
  Presidents
J. A. Sabouraud – Secretary/Treasurer
M. A. Delattre – Joint Secretary
Committee Members: Mme Blain, Mme de Courtil-
  loles, Messrs Pezet, Dr Giralt, Ch Douillard,
  Montenot, Nicolosi. Mme Senac-Lagrange, who
  has resigned, has been replaced by Mme Frei.
  Mme de Courtilloles has also resigned and been
  replaced by Mlle Lamazou-Betheder.

And now it remains only to sum up.

Our breeding of large and small Pyreneans has increased. We have seen our dogs present at nearly all the
shows, not always very numerous, but of quality. In
particular we would mention two excellent champions
shown at Tarbes in May 1966.

Notes of the judge, M. Ch Douillard

Male Champion Class

Excellent – *Mouky de Pontoise*. A well known dog full of
great qualities. Well boned, good pigmentation, beautiful expression and above all, this dog has the rare quality
of having an open, gay and trustworthy character. Moreover, he combines perfectly the qualities of strength and
elegance, such a rare combination in our males.

Female Champion Class

Excellent – *Micoune du Comté de Foix*. This well known
bitch is full of great qualities and approaches perfection.
The cup for the best dog or bitch offered by the Réunion
des Amateurs de Chiens Pyrénéens and the Harper-
Trois-Fontaines silver cup brought *Mouky de Pontoise* and
Micoune du Comté de Foix face to face. Keen competition
between two high class dogs, and my choice could
perhaps be reversed another time.

Indeed, for pure beauty *Micoune* is unbeatable, but I
wanted to honour *Mouky* for his temperament and his

excellent open and gay character, of which I have spoken and which one rarely finds. I also wanted to honour this dog for his physical elegance and vivacity, which is a change from the all too numerous large males who are heavy and fat, and seem incapable of covering 1 km at a trot.

New affixes were registered:

De Gerbanères belonging to Mme Janick Prat. *Du Pech a'Ajteroc* belonging to M. Corretja.
M. Robert Coffunier's kennel. *Des Salissaudres* belonging to Mme Sallé for the mountain dogs. Mlle Bonniol de Guieste's *Du Chateau de Réveillon.* M. Germain Latapie's *Du Lavedan.* M. Guy Mansencal's *De l'Estaubé.* M. A. Perrot's *Du Hic.*

During these latter years we have seen several dogs have a good career. We shall shortly make special mention of the de Pontoise establishment. We would point out the progress and remarkable success of the *Comté de Foix* breeding, the *Josse* of M. Corretja, and the old *du Jaout* and *de Poeymayou* breedings. We regret the disappearance of the beautiful specimens of M. Collongue of *de la Cime d'Azur*. Let us note very recently the good intentions of M. Severac in the Var and, in the Isere, an important line of Sheepdogs, with the affix *De Golden Roc,* belonging to M. Chausson.

Among the Sheepdogs, the maintenance in the first rank of the old kennel *de la Miche;* the demise of *de la Pastorale;* the brilliant career of the *de Fleurac* dogs, of whom *Fine Mouche* was the grand star, thought to be nearly perfect by every judge. We record with pleasure the great activity of the kennel *du Hic,* orientated upon the working dog.

We marvel at the success of M. Delattre, success due to his sense of breeding and to his experience, learned from the best models.

Starting out in 1933, he had the chance to receive and to follow the principles of the great master, M. Senac-Lagrange. Following advice received, he knew how to study his selection, which led him to success. 31 Champions of France, several international champions.

12 Grand Prizes of honour from the President of the Republic. And he continues, profiting from his reputation, to export dogs throughout the world. His kennel is composed of 20 adults, of which several are in retirement.

There is another breeder whose success is as great, living in a great country where dogs are loved even more than they are here – Mme Harper Trois-Fontaines.

It was in 1929 that Mme Harper first met the Pyrenean Mountain Dog. In 1933 she introduced the first dogs into England and had several disappointments with the quarantine. The first dogs died there. One cannot easily explain such a rigorous regulation for allowing dogs entry into England. Our Pyreneans, which need so much affection, die there of a broken heart.

She introduced into her breeding *Kop de Careil*, bred by M. Jemming out of his bitch *Mireille*, daughter of champion *Gazost de Betpoey*, of which the sire was *Patou de Careil* son of the well-known *Rip de la Noé*. After that she took eleven dogs and bitches to England, chosen from amongst the best blood lines of France, which were *Ariel de Soum*, champion *Gazost de Betpoey*, international champions *Estate* and *Estagel d'Argelès*, and champion *Norah de Careil*.

It was with the offspring of these champions that she founded her de Fontenay kennel, which she was able to preserve during the war with great sacrifices and great difficulties.

In 1946 the breed was recognised by the English Kennel Club and since then, up to 1958, she has produced 28 champions in this kennel, which is one of the most modern in England.

She has also gained a reputation in every country in the world.

The English Pyrenean Club was founded in 1936 and in 1958 totalled 80 members. Mme Harper came back many times in search of fresh blood. One of the sons of *Kop de Careil* had six of his sons and daughters become champions. Since 1947 she has bred 28 champions.

In 1947 Mme Harper, having been asked to judge in America, took back a dog *Basquaerie Perce Neige* who, mated to a bitch who was a daughter of *Kop de Careil* and *Nethou de Langladure*, produced her best dog, *President de Fontenay*, who was 24 times Best of Breed and was considered by many judges to be the most beautiful Pyrenean in the world. In her search for dogs in the Pyrenees, she had the advantage of obtaining the help of M. Senac-Lagrange, without whom she would have risked making mistakes at the beginning, knowing neither the vendors nor the origins of the dogs that were offered to her.

It is interesting to re-read certain of the impressions brought back by M. Senac-Lagrange who, in November 1951, had been asked to judge at the L.K.A. show, the most important show in England after Crufts, which totalled 6,295 dogs and 72 judges. He came back with excellent memories, enchanted by the way in which he had been received with respect and friendliness.

Mme Harper invited him to visit her beautiful house and her magnificent kennel. This is what we were able to extract from this very important report.

> I had 75 dogs to judge. I found the Pyreneans in England better than I had hoped. Our best dogs are as good as theirs and perhaps even beat them. I did not see the equivalent of *Sultan* owned by M. Collongue, but on average the dogs seem superior to those of French breeding. Most of the subjects, dogs and bitches, are large. I even examined one dog who was 80 cm (31 in) at the shoulders. One senses that the dogs are well nourished, some even being too well fed. In general pigmentation is correct. The English seem to have understood the importance of pigment and amongst their recent imports are two strongly coloured dogs. The fullness of the skulls is fairly constant and the cephalic pattern satisfactory. The two most common faults can be found in the eyelids and the muzzles. Too many eyelids are round and loose, the result of a too plentiful diet. As for the muzzles, they are the victims of a fad, which I can verify without being able to explain it, which incites the English judges to favour rectangular profiles, and it therefore follows that the English bred

Pyreneans have an excess of flews and consequently of dewlaps. Although I did not find the expression as intensely developed as in certain French dogs, most of the dogs presented it in what might be described as an attenuate form. I noticed only two dogs in which it was totally lacking.

In short, the breeding of Pyreneans in England is on the right track. This is largely due to the efforts of the president of the English club, Mme Harper, who knew how to combine and utilise the bloods of the best French breedings. A discreet use of American blood, itself an issue of our greatest bloodlines, came to reinforce the quality of the English breeding. We would state without comment, that it has emigrated nearly everywhere, both in and out of Europe, as far as Australia and India.

These results have been obtained in a relatively short time as there was a good start. Breeding was started on a solid basis, without worrying about the sacrifices inherent in every new enterprise, and which sooner or later should find its reward.

How has the breed evolved since 1951? M. Delattre attended Cruft's in 1965 and 1966. He saw 56 Pyreneans being shown, and in his report he says:

> I must recognise that in our breed, the English breeders have absolutely no reason to envy us. The males were almost all of excellent quality. There were seven who, without doubt merited the C.C., but only one could have it. It was a delicate task for the judge, Mrs Passini-Birkett. If three of the bitches dominated the others, they were nevertheless as a whole much better than those shown last year. The English do not scorn any advice which one is able to give them, and one breeder asked me, in introducing me to numerous exhibitors, to kindly indicate to her the faults which I could find with their dogs, thus proving their desire to see not only the good qualities.

In finishing this chapter we would like to send our thanks and congratulations to Mme Harper for her excellent work.

We would also note an important breeding in America started in 1932. The first Pyrenean bought by Mr Crane for his breeding stock in America was *Urdos de Soum*, born at Lourdes on 20th May, 1931, son of *Toy de Soum* out of *Lutour de Langladure*. Following this Mr Crane bought dogs from the following French kennels: *de la Noé, Betpouey, la Morinière, du Pic du Jer, de Careil, de Soum, de Langladure, d'Argelès* etc. However, we have no information on the evolution and the importance of this American breeding.

A club for this dog exists in America, whose secretary is Miss Alton Kiborg. There is another in California, but we lack any further information.

Conclusion

In the course of this book we may have made several oversights and omissions. We beg to be excused – this was unintentional.

One last word. Pyreneans give their heart to their master. They wish to be paid in return. They must be treated as friends, if not as members of the family. Lack of confidence and affection can make them dangerously indifferent.

Confirmation

1 Regulations

The instructions of the Minister of Agriculture concerning confirmation require all animals capable of maintaining and improving the breed i.e. conforming to the Standard, to be confirmed.

Confirmation should not be confused with the selection of the best animals for breeding. It is up to the Clubs to examine the average quality of their breed, and to determine access to confirmation at this level.

For the selection of their breed, they have scope to emphasise their 'Recommended Subjects' and the 'Best Reproducers'.

Confirmation gives access to the final registration – the French Register of Origin. This Register is currently 'open' for all breeds, and it is possible for certain subjects to have access to final registration through the 'Initial Title'.

The minimum age for confirmation is the age of admission to Dog Shows. Clubs which consider it opportune to fix a later date for the examination for confirmation should request the Société Centrale Canine to fix the age for showing to correspond with that which they consider good for confirmation.

Confirmation can be carried out either at a show, or on presentation or in a competition, or at the request of the Club, by a Qualified Judge or Probationary Judge, or by an examiner nominated by the Club.

Subsequently, with certain breeds, confirmation is

completed by verification of natural qualities.

All Qualified Judges or Probationary Judges with the Société Centrale Canine are recognised as being able to award confirmation.

All judges of a country which is a member of the Cynological Federation or Members of a similar federation, are authorised to award confirmation, subject to the agreement of the Club concerned.

In case of need, the Clubs can appoint examiners who are not judges, but who are capable of carrying out the confirmation examination. In this case, they should advise the Société Centrale Canine of their decision. These examiners can not in any circumstances be referred to as 'Judges'.

This measure is designed to allow breeders to have their dogs confirmed outside the show season.

It is up to Clubs to explain to all Judges, whether French or Foreign, their directives on the points entailing a refusal of confirmation, which they should apply.

Complaints of any exaggeration either one way or another, can be taken up with the Société Centrale Canine.

In the same way, when giving instructions to Judges, Clubs should keep strictly to the framework of the instructions of the Ministry of Agriculture as well as to the regulations of the Société Centrale Canine concerning confirmation.

In case of non-confirmation, the owner of a dog which is not confirmed can appeal to the Société Centrale Canine within 6 months.

Equally, the Breed Clubs can appeal to the Société Centrale Canine against a confirmation which they do not consider to be justified, and this must be done within two months.

2 Formalities

The Confirmation examination should be requested by the owner of the dog on a special form which is divided into two parts:

one headed 'Request for Confirmation Examination' the other 'Certificate of Confirmation'

These two parts should be completed carefully by the owner before being handed to the Judge with the Birth Certificate or Certificate of Parentage of the dog being presented.

After the confirmation examination, two cases have to be considered.

1. *If the dog is confirmed:* the owner sends the Société Centrale Canine the Certificate of Confirmation signed by the Judge, together with the Birth Certificate or Certificate of Parentage of the dog which has been confirmed. After verification, the Société Centrale Canine sends the Confirmation Certificates signed by the Judges for the approval of the Breed Club. These Certificates should be returned within 8 days to the Société Centrale Canine, who waits for them before proceeding with the final entry in the French Register of Origin and the issue of the Final Pedigree of the dogs confirmed.

2. *If the dog is not confirmed:* In cases of non-confirmation, the Judge who has refused confirmation should himself return the form requesting the confirmation examination to the Société Centrale Canine. He must specify the reasons for non-confirmation and he must advise the owner of the dog of them. In its turn the Société Centrale Canine advises the Breed Club of the reasons. In the case of foreign judges, the Society which has organised the examination acts as a substitute for them in sending to the Société Centrale Canine the request for the confirmation examination for dogs which they have refused.

The endorsement of non-confirmation is placed on the Declaration of Birth form in the Register of Young Dogs.

Dogs Born Between 1st January 1962 and 31st December 1963

During this transitory period the ordinary pedigrees were issued with an endorsement stating that for breeding, these dogs would have to be confirmed.

After the confirmation examination, for which the formalities were the same as above, the Société Centrale Canine marked, by perforation, the endorsement 'confirmed' or 'not confirmed'.

The age of admission to shows for Pyrenean dogs is 12 – 24 months for the Young Dog class.

Age of confirmation: from 12 months.

Very Important

Litters from breeding stock which have not reached the age for confirmation are not allowed to be registered.

Appendix

The Champions

All dogs can be entered at shows, but only those who have a French Certificate of Origin can have their wins confirmed.

The right to the title of 'National Champion' goes to dogs who have obtained three first prizes with CAC'S at three international shows organised by the Société Centrale Canine or by an affiliated society, under three different judges, of which at least one was at the Paris show.

To obtain the title of International Beauty Champion, CACIB's, the dogs must have obtained four international CACIB's in three different countries under three different judges, irrespective of the number of competitors. Note that in both cases if the CACIB is given to a dog that is already a champion, the reserve CACIB is counted as the CACIB's: and similarly for the CAC's.

There is no need to say that if one wishes to enter a dog at a show, one should take a clean dog, trained to know how to show himself correctly, calmly accepting the judge's examination. Above all, take care not to bath him during the days just before the show – bathing spoils the coat.